BLACK GIRL IN A CORPORATE WORLD

Written by:

Sultana Sams

ACKNOWLEDGEMENTS

I am so thrilled to have completed this book. Work discrimination in the workplace is not discussed often because people don't want to get fired or get in trouble. I, as well as many others, have went through this and it needed to be addressed. I want to thank everyone who shared their story of work discrimination with me. You are not alone and together we will keep fighting for equal rights in the workplace and everywhere else.

<u>Chapter 1</u>

Charity was at work working on a big case. She'd spent countless hours researching the case. She had a meeting today with Mr. Peters, the lawyer she worked under. There was a lot of information that would help his case. She loved helping clients when she believed they were innocent. Though she was a paralegal, she planned to be a lawyer one day. The work she put in as a paralegal was more than the lawyers over the case had put in. It was her who did all the research and found all the facts for the case.

"Charity, can I see you for a minute?" Mr. Peters said as he stuck his head in her office.

"Sure. Do you want to go over my findings for the case early?" she asked him.

"We'll do that later. I just need a quick moment. Come to my office."

"Ok. I'll be there in two minutes," Charity replied as he exited. She pressed save on the notes that she was typing up and shut down her computer.

As she entered the office, she noticed Katie was also in there. Katie had been with the company for six months as a Receptionist. She'd been studying to be a paralegal and was almost finished with school.

"Hi," Charity muttered to Katie and Mr. Peters as she wondered what this meeting was about.

"How's everything going with the research?" Mr. Peters asked.

"Great! I found some interesting facts that will definitely help the case. I thought you didn't want to go over that now though?" Charity was baffled and struggled not to show the puzzling look on her face. Hadn't he said earlier they would go over that later?

"I don't. It can wait."

"Ok," Charity asserted. So, what the hell do you want? She kept this thought to herself.

"Katie is almost done with school and she's graduating at the top of her class. I'd like to bring her with me to the court date next week."

"I thought I'd finally get to sit with you?" Charity asked. She'd helped him win numerous cases but had always sat in the audience in court or wasn't able to attend court at all. There was always an excuse, or he would give her something to do at the office. She was excited to finally sit to the table with him.

"You will. I just wanted to show her the entire process and let her sit with me."

"But I've never gotten to sit with you even after all the research. I was excited to get the chance. And I worked really hard and late nights."

"You've been doing great work. You'll get the chance real soon," Mr. Peters said, brushing her off as he always did.

Charity was quiet. She didn't want to say the wrong things and she knew it was possible because she was getting pissed. The notepad she'd carried into the office slipped out of her hand because she'd been squeezing it tightly trying to control her feelings. How does the receptionist get to sit at his table before her? As if it wasn't obvious.

"Go over your notes with Katie during our meeting slot so that she'll be briefed on what's going on. She can also add her own research in the next few days."

"I can assure you there won't be much to add. I've been working hard and staying late. I've found some really great things to ensure the case goes our way. I'd actually prefer going over some things with you since we've been working on this a while. Things have to be presented a certain way to make it make sense," Charity told Mr. Peters.

"It won't be necessary to go over it with me. She'll go over it with me," Mr. Peters said.

"But-," Charity couldn't even finish her sentence before being interrupted.

"That will be all. I'm really busy today," Mr. Peters said, dismissing her rudely.

Charity glared at him and his bald ass head. He'd turned to Katie and was smiling. Looking up at her he said, "Ok, you can go now. It's a busy day for us all. Katie will meet with you at our meeting time."

Charity said nothing. She just turned and walked out.

She went back into her office and shut the door. She was pissed! She'd been working with Mr. Peters for over two years. Yet, he'd never let her sit next to him in court. She'd been to a handful of trials but only sat in the audience. He'd always had excuses or had her busy when she wanted to go watch the case. How can a paralegal do their job if they couldn't hear the whole trial? Still, she'd researched and

worked countless hours, making sure he had enough evidence and facts to win his cases. Now the receptionist was going to sit with him? Katie hadn't done much real paralegal work. She did some simple research for the other lawyers when she needed it to count as research hours for school but that was about it. The bitch wasn't even finished with school yet. But, since she was a white girl, she would get to leap way past Charity in her career.

Chapter 2

"Hello?" Janae was just getting in her car as her cell phone rang. It was her best friend, Charity.

"Hey girl. You done got off?"

"Yea I'm leaving now. What's up?" Janae asked her friend, who sounded down.

"Just blowed about work. Mr. Peters is letting that bitch Katie sit with him in court instead of me."

"What? You've been waiting for this! Katie? Ain't she the receptionist bitch?"

"Exactly! I need a drink!" Charity said.

"Let's make margaritas. I'll bring everything to your house. I'm headed to the store, then I'll come to you."

"That's why we're besties!" Charity smiled.

After hanging up with Janae, Charity made a quick dinner for them. She started making shrimp fettuccini. There was no garlic bread, so she decided to use biscuits. It wasn't long before the doorbell rang.

"Hey girl," Janae said with bags in her hand. She followed Charity to the kitchen. "You cooking? Yay!"

"Yea, we can't drink on an empty stomach. Besides, I needed to do something cause I'm pissed."

"Yea, that's wrong how your boss is handling things. We all know it's because she is white. Nothing else makes sense. Honestly, I never understood why you weren't always in court with him in the first place. It's as if he's hiding you from the world."

"Right!" Charity declared. "I hate to think it has to do with race, but what else could it be? I work damn hard. I barely have a life because I'm always working. It's not fair!" Tears were trying to creep into her eyes.

"You're right. It's not fair! People don't want to believe it but unless they're in that type of environment, they won't understand. I love my job as a marketing assistant, and I feel my bosses respect my work. But, the company has over seventy people employed and there are only three black people. That is not a good look. I just continue to work hard to show them that our people can get the job done too. I'm hoping they'll hire more of us down the line."

"That's a damn shame," Charity stated as she sipped her drink. "We got to work harder than them and still get fewer steps ahead.

"Yes. Truth is, I stopped wearing braids when I got this job. I felt they'd prefer I wear my real hair. I also felt that it made me look more professional."

"That's some sad shit," Charity said. "Why the hell can't we just be treated like humans?"

Janae just shook her head. They sipped and continued talking about their jobs and other things for a few hours before Janae went home.

~

The next few days were a blur at work. Charity briefed Katie as instructed and continued her duties as usual. She'd hoped to get a quick meeting with Mr. Peters, but they'd all been busy, and she decided she would deal with it next week.

Happy to leave work, she entered the elevator. She worked on the 5th floor, so she pressed 1 to get to the exit at the lobby. Riding alone, she stared at the elevator doors. She didn't expect it to stop, but it did on the 3rd floor. A tall, medium-brown complexioned man with a dark blue suit on walked in the elevator. His suit was tailored to fit him, so Charity assumed it was expensive. He smiled at her, flashing pearly white teeth. Then, he glanced to make sure the button for the first floor was already pressed.

"Hey beautiful, I'm Ashton," the guy said, extending his hand to Charity. He looked at her like she was candy. She wore a simple blue dress that she dressed up with her black suit jacket, which sat just above her butt. Her butt wasn't huge, but it sat up nicely. She was a tad bit darker in complexion than him with cute dimples. She only stood about 5 foot, 5 inches and he looked at least 6 feet.

Surprised to see a handsome and nicely dressed black man, she just stared at him. Before she said anything, the elevator door opened.

"After you," Ashton told her as she exited the elevator and he followed her. He continued walking with her out of the building. "So, are you going to tell me your name?"

For some reason Charity felt nervous having this man walking near her. Maybe because he was so fine. "Sorry I'm Charity."

"You're racing out of here. What's the rush?"

"It's been a rough week at work and I'm just ready to go home," Charity continued walking towards her car as they talked.

"I understand," Ashton said. "Unfortunately, I'll be working at home most of the weekend. Any chance I can take you out for dinner tomorrow night?"

Charity blushed. She needed a distraction. Work had made it too busy for her to date, but she needed to get out. "Ok. Sure."

Ashton smiled, and they exchanged numbers. He walked her to her car in the parking lot before heading to his black 2020 Mercedes-Benz and heading home. Pulling up to his house, he parked in his driveway. He'd just purchased his home last year. It had four bedrooms and three baths. Yet, he lived alone. Opening his own law firm at the age 35 kept him busy. As he entered his empty house, he looked around. "Maybe it's time for a family." He'd never thought this way before, but for some reason it was on his mind heavy today. Was it because of the beautiful young lady he'd met in the elevator?

<u>**Chapter 3**</u>

Charity and Janae were spending Friday night catching up with the Real Housewives of Atlanta on TV and drinking Patron. They were both happy about it being the weekend.

"I see your hair freshly braided. Looking good," Charity told Janae, referring to her box braids.

"Yes, our talk inspired me to get the hairstyle I've wanted for a while. Braids are so damn convenient. And I'm excited because today, I pitched a big ad campaign at work," Janae said. "Well, I pitched it to my boss. She's been so helpful in my career. She is one of the few people at the company who doesn't see color. So, I decided wearing braids won't be an issue."

"That's great! Yea of course every white person is not prejudiced. It's always just a few bad apples. My boss just prefers helping the white, eye candy over me. There are others at my job that's nice," Charity said.

"Yes, I'm so thrilled. She's going to help me pitch to her boss. If my ad gets chosen, it will come with a big bonus and I'm sure a job promotion."

"That would be great!" Charity was happy for her friend. "Let's take a shot to that!"

A couple of hours passed before Charity's phone rang. By this time, she'd been drinking a bit too much.

"Hello?" She said without looking at the caller ID.

"Hey. Is this a good time?" It was Ashton.

"Who is this?" Charity asked. She knew who it was but was surprised he was calling already.

"Ashton. From the elevator at work. I guess you have a lot of male callers," he laughed.

"No, I don't," Charity smiled hard as she talked to him. "Work has me too busy. We were drinking and I had to think about it for a second."

Janae looked at Charity smiling, "Put it on speakerphone." Charity obliged.

"*We* were drinking?" Ashton asked. It was apparent that he wanted to know who "we" were.

"Yes, we. Me and my best friend," Charity told him while Janae listened in.

"Oh, cool!" Ashton sounded relieved. "So, you do have some sort of life besides work?"

"She really doesn't," Janae chimed in, then laughed.

Ashton laughed too. "Well, are we still on for tomorrow night?"

"Yes, y'all are," Janae said.

"I can speak for myself," Charity blushed. She took the phone off the speaker. "Yes, we're still on if work doesn't have you too busy."

"Oh, I won't let it," he responded.

Charity couldn't control the blushing. "Well, good then."

"So go back to having fun with your best friend. I'll see you tomorrow."

"Ok," Charity said, then he hung up.

As soon as she hung up, Janae stared at her. "Well, damn! When were you going to tell me about this dude?"

"I was just about to tell you in a few. He works in my building. We met in the elevator."

"And your boring ass agreed to go out with him? I'm proud of you. He must be fine."

Charity laughed. "He is nice looking. He's also a lawyer."

"Wow. Love at first sight," Janae said.

"Girl hush. Ain't like you got a man either!"

Janae laughed. "I know, but I have been on dates and even got me some more recently than you."

"That's 'cause you're a hoe on the low," Charity joked while clapping her hands and laughing.

Janae laughed too. They continued sipping and talking. Charity's job wasn't going right, so maybe her love life finally would. Janae's job situation seemed to be on the way to getting better, and Charity was happy for her friend. Her occupation wasn't an easy one, and Charity remembered her working hard in school and work. It wasn't long before the drinks kicked in and they both fell asleep on Charity's couch.

~

It was 5:15 am when Janae opened her eyes and realized she'd never gone home. She saw the time on her phone. Seeing Charity still snoring peacefully, she decided not to wake her up. She put on her shoes and quietly grabbed her coat, purse and keys. It was still dark outside. She unlocked her car with the key fob and got in and drove home to get in her own bed.

Hearing the door closed, Charity opened her eyes and looked up just as Janae was leaving. She got up and walked to the door. Janae was pulling off when she opened it, so she shut her door back and went into her kitchen. She fixed some coffee, then cleaned up the mess they'd made in her living room. Going to her room, she showered then got in her bed. She'd planned on going back to sleep but couldn't. She thought about her date later with Ashton. After turning to the ID channel and watching a woman kill her husband, she finally went back to sleep after 7:00 am.

She'd slept a while and got up to the sound of her phone ringing. Grabbing her phone, she saw that it was Janae.

"Hello," Charity mumbled groggily.

"Don't tell me you're still asleep. It's lunchtime!"

"I woke up when you left, cleaned up, showered then went back to sleep." Looking at the clock, it read 12:32. "I needed some rest anyway."

"You did," Janae agreed, "continue resting but not too long. Remember your date tonight."

Charity thought about Ashton. She smiled. "Oh, yea. Well let me get myself together. You gone stop by later? Help me find an outfit?"

"Sure, it's not like I have anything else to do."

Charity hung up then looked at her phone. She had a good morning text from Ashton. It had been around 9.

She texted back, *"Good morning or shall I say good afternoon. Sorry I was asleep."*

About 10 minutes later, he called.

"Sleep? It must be nice to have that luxury," Ashton said once she answered the phone.

"It rarely happens. I'm always up briefing for a case, but this weekend I'm choosing to relax."

"I understand," Ashton said. "I was up a little early as well briefing for a case, but it gives me pleasure knowing that I'll be seeing you later."

"It gives me pleasure too," Charity said. No one hadn't had her blushing like this in a long while.

They chatted for a few minutes and then she told him to get back to work and she'll see him later. She then fixed herself a sandwich for lunch, started her weekend

chores and lounged around a little while.

<u>Chapter 4</u>

Dinner was nice. Ashton insisted on picking her up. They went to a restaurant known for mouth-watering steaks. Inside was dim and romantic lighting. They sat by a window and enjoyed the view of the lake nearby.

"This is so nice. Thank you," Charity said.

"You're welcome. It seemed like you needed a relaxing night out."

"I did," Charity admitted.

After both ordering steaks, baked potato and salad, the waitress brought them their drinks. They were drinking wine. Charity wanted to start off light. It didn't take long for Charity to loosen up. She ended up telling Ashton everything about the job situation.

"Wow. That's a lot. And that's not right."

"I know. I felt like being up under Mr. Peters would teach me a lot. He's the reason I started applying to law schools. He promised to show me the ropes but barely wants me in the courtroom."

Ashton looked perplexed. It was obvious that he didn't like the situation that she was in but didn't want to overstep. "You'll still be a great lawyer so continue to apply for schools. You can even start some classes online. Experience is everything and you have that. Obviously, you're good at what you do, or he wouldn't have kept you around. Just let him know how you feel. We can't be scared to stand up for ourselves."

"You're so right. I have to stand up for myself or I'll end up being miserable."

"We can't have that. You're too beautiful and smart to be miserable."

"Thank you," Charity smiled.

He told her he'd been a lawyer for 5 years. He was 32 years old. He'd also worked under someone after his internship, but it didn't work out, so he used his savings and a loan to open his own practice. It started with him working from home, but he'd recently rented an office in the building she worked. So far it was only him and his receptionist.

"That is so wonderful. A young black man who has his own law firm." Charity was impressed.

"Thank you. It is impressive to meet a young, beautiful black paralegal who will become a lawyer one day.

Charity blushed again. She didn't know if the wine was making her comfortable or him. They ate and talked the night away. After dinner, he walked her to her door, and they kissed passionately. Being a great gentleman, he left after she went into the house. They both spent the night thinking about their amazing date. It was nice out, so he took her out to eat by the beach. Since they'd arrived well before their reservations, they took a walk along the pier and talked. The view of the water was so beautiful. They'd been so caught up walking and talking, they arrived a few minutes late to the restaurant. The restaurant had big see-through windows that looked out onto the beach water. The beautiful and relaxing scenery made the date feel romantic. They both lay in bed reminiscing about how much they enjoyed their time with each other.

~

The next day was Sunday. Charity's plan was to stay in bed all day. Ashton was working as usual. She would usually be working too but since she'd briefed Katie there wasn't anything else for her to do. The court date was next week, and Katie would be sitting in, so it was now Katie's problem. Around lunchtime, she went into the kitchen to fix a sandwich and a salad. It was unusual sitting home doing nothing, so she sat in front of her TV. She'd just turned to Netflix to catch up on what she'd been missing while working so much when the doorbell rang. She opened without looking, which was a bad habit. There was a white guy standing at the door with flowers in his hand.

"Charity?" he asked.

"Yes?"

"These are for you. Have a nice day," he handed her the flowers and walked away.

Shutting her door, she looked at the red roses. They were beautiful. They were already in a nice vase. She sat them on her coffee table and grabbed the card.

"Thanks for a beautiful dinner. Hope you like roses." It was signed by Ashton. Charity blushed. It had been a while since she'd dated. Ashton was seeming like a really nice guy. Smelling the roses, she smiled. This was what she needed after everything she was dealing with at work. She thanked him by text, and he told her she was very welcome and deserving. Excited she dialed Janae.

"Hey girl," Janae said. "How was your date last night?"

Charity told her about the nice date and the flowers.

"Wow," Janae said, "seems like he's a keeper."

"It's new so I don't know but he is a much-needed distraction with everything going on at work."

"Yes, he is. Does he have a brother?" Janae joked.

Charity laughed.

"I gotta call you back later," Janae said. "I'm getting my hair braided."

"You getting braids? I thought you liked to wear your real hair straight for work. Don't your light skin ass like to blend in with the white people you work with."

Janae laughed. "Yea at first but since they like my work I'm getting my braids back. They're convenient and it's getting cold."

"So true," Charity said. "Hit me later then. I'm going to Netflix and chill."

"Ok. Talk to you later," Janae said then they hung up.

Charity spent the rest of the day watching an exciting series on Netflix. She spoke with Ashton several times throughout the day too. He had a case in court that he was preparing for, but he made time to check in on her and she appreciated it.

<u>Chapter 5</u>

Janae walked into work with new confidence. She was proud of her ad pitch. She set up in her office and prepared to meet with her boss. They were going to go over pitching her ad to her boss's boss and the big client this week. A lot was at stake, so she planned to make a good impression. Once done preparing, she looked at her watch and noticed it was just a few minutes until meeting in the conference room. She gathered her things and walked down to where the meeting was being held.

"Good morning," Janae greeted her boss as she walked in with a big smile and pep in her step.

"Good morning," her boss Patricia said. Janae noticed a puzzled look on her face.

"Is everything ok?"

"Yes," Patricia said. "I was just surprised to see your new hairdo. What are those called?"

"Braids," Janae told her smiling. "They're convenient. I don't have to curl my hair in the morning and that extra time is much needed." Janae laughed expecting her boss to laugh too but there was a weird vibe.

Changing the subject, Janae put her folders of information on the table. "I did a PowerPoint that I think you'll love."

"Great," Patricia said.

Janae went over the PowerPoint with Patricia. It made the points they'd talked about plus more points that were very intriguing. It was obvious Patricia was impressed.

"What do you think? Do you think it's too much? Maybe I need to change some things?" Janae was excited but willing to listen to constructive criticism.

"I actually think it is wonderful," Patricia said.

"So, did you set up the meeting for us tomorrow? My first big pitch with my own idea. I'm excited."

"Yes, I set up the meeting, but I think it would be better if I pitched it to the client. Don't worry. You will still get all the credit, but they know me and are more comfortable with me."

"I know they're comfortable with you that's why I want you by my side. But we agreed since the idea was all mine that I would pitch it. You said it would be better if I showed my face and talent more instead of just being the brains behind the ads and marketing." Janae didn't understand what Patricia was saying. It was her idea.

Patricia sighed. "We've been working together for a while and I love your work. I love your personality too. It brightens my day all the time."

"Ok," Janae said. She didn't know what else to say. She was trying to figure out where her boss was going with this.

"I promise I don't want to offend you," Patricia was twiddling her thumbs at this point. "Is it possible to take your braids out before tomorrow's meeting and wear your regular style?"

"My braids out? Why?"

"Well, you look more professional without them. That's why I recommended you do the pitch. I like how you carry yourself and your professionalism."

"I still will carry myself the same and be very professional. My hair is neat and pulled back, so it doesn't look wild. I'm not understanding," Janae was getting upset. She was beginning to see what was going on.

"Look. I promise you will still get the same credit if I pitch it. I just thought your first impression to the client would be better. That's all. You're smart, beautiful, hardworking and professional. I can never take that away from you. I'll pitch it. We know they'll love it, and they'll meet you at another meeting." Patricia looked at Janae. She was hoping that she wasn't offending her.

"Is it because I'm black? You don't like my black hairstyle?" Janae asked. She tried her best not to have an attitude, but she thought about Charity's job situation and how she thought her company was so different when it came to black people.

"You've always been black, and I've still always liked you. I've always been honest about what you needed to do to get ahead, and you listened and worked hard. Now you're being awarded this perfect opportunity. Are you going to ruin it because of an urban hairstyle?" Patricia asked. Personally, she really did like Janae. It didn't matter her color because she portrayed herself professionally. But, she'd been in business for years and it was hard enough for her to get Janae this opportunity. People didn't want to see black faces; however, since Janae was bright skinned, wore her own real hair usually, she felt she could fit in. Of course, she wouldn't tell Janae all this. She knew race was a sensitive subject.

"Urban hairstyle?" Janae questioned. "Is that how you see me? Urban? I work just as hard as you and anyone else here and you want to label me because I like a convenient and neat hairstyle?" Proud of herself, she remained calm and professional. She refused to let the angry black woman's label get on her.

Patricia sighed. "I'm not labeling you. I like you a lot and I'm rooting for you. I promise I want to see you win and move up in the company. Your hair looks great. I'm just speaking from my boss's and our big client's perspective."

"Oh, so you think they'll have a problem with my hair? I'll look too black to them?"

"No. That's not it. It's all about professional appearance and since this is your first big pitch, I was just giving some advice. It's up to you. I'm not trying to offend you."

"Well, if it's up to me, I'd like to keep my new hairstyle and do the pitch myself with you as planned. It's just hair. I get where you're going with professionalism, but I still look professional." Janae showed Patricia her outfit when she said that. She had on a two-piece black pants suit. Her brown, black and red blouse matched her brown heels. Her box braids were pulled back into a ball, just like she'd worn her real hair at times. She wasn't seeing the problem. Patricia was overreacting in her opinion.

Patricia sighed. "You're right. I'm sorry. The meeting is at 1:00 tomorrow. Be ready."

"I will," Janae smiled. She was irritated but wasn't going to show it. She planned on killing the presentation tomorrow and showing Patricia what she could do. After that, she knew Patricia would relax.

"Ok great. Well, feel free to take the rest of the day off if you want. You deserve it. And I want to apologize about the hair. I was just being cautious. This client is extremely important, and the firm is going to make a lot of money off them.”

“I’m going to make sure you make that money,” Janae said. She smiled, though she still felt bothered. “I’ll go home and look over everything again. Earlier, I emailed you the presentation and notes. Look over it and let me know if you have any questions or want to add anything.”

“I will, but I know I won’t because your pitch is perfect,” Patricia smiled, “now enjoy the rest of your day.”

“Thank you,” Janae walked out of the conference room back to her office. Shutting the door, she spent half an hour answering emails and making sure everything was in place. Then, taking her boss’s suggestion, she grabbed her coat and left for the day. It was lunchtime and her growling stomach reminded her of it.

Leaving the office, she called Charity, but there was no answer. She grabbed some food and waited until Charity was off to call her again. Going home and sitting on the couch didn't sound bad especially how she was feeling.

~

Charity was just at work to be there. Mr. Peters would be in court all week. She would be working on trivial cases. The big case was at the courthouse. It was almost the end of the day when Mr. Peters came back into the office. He peeked into Charity's office.

"Hi. Anything I need to know? Anything interesting happened here today?" he asked her.

"No," Charity said. It still upset her about not being in court.

"Do you want to know about court?" Mr. Peters was surprised she hadn't asked him a million questions as she'd usually do when he came from the courthouse.

"I'm sure our receptionist can tell me when I see her."

Mr. Peters knew where this was going. "I know you're disappointed. You're up next. Maybe you can come sit and watch court tomorrow. At least part of the time."

Charity genuinely wanted to sit next to him not in the audience, but she didn't want to make a fuss and lose her job. "I'll see. If we don't get too busy here."

"Great," Mr. Peters smiled and walked off. He didn't want Charity to be upset with him. He knew she was smart and capable. Katie had the look that he felt was needed. Plus, her family had money and they were good clients. It really wasn't anything personal. It was merely business to him.

Chapter 6

Charity went home and plopped on the couch. Ashton was working late. He'd told her he would call her later. Looking at her phone, she saw she'd missed a couple of calls from Janae. She called her back.

"Hey, girl I meant to call you back from earlier," Charity told her friend.

"I know your ass was probably talking to Ashton on the phone," Janae joked.

"Yea and at work sulking."

"I know the feeling. That's why I've been calling," Janae told her sounding down. She told Charity what was going on at work.

"Wow," Charity was shocked. "I never expected that with Patricia. We're in the south and I know there are a lot of undercover prejudice people, but your boss seemed cool."

"Well, there are only a few black faces in the company. That should have given me a clue. I was in fairytale land thinking my work would speak for itself."

"Your work does speak for itself. Don't let anyone take that away from you. You work hard and you are good at what you do," Charity told Janae. Her friend was usually excited about work and she didn't like that she was doubting herself.

"I know. I just get sick of the prejudice shit. She told me in so many words that the people at the presentation wouldn't like my braids because they were urban. I guess she wanted me to wear my own straight hair as I usually did. And to be honest, the reason I wore my hair straight and natural was because I didn't want to be judged. But after being there for a while, I didn't think it would be an issue. You know how much I missed getting my braids," Janae cried her friend. "Wanna help me take them out tonight?"

"You are not taking your hair out tonight. You paid for your style and you shall keep it. I'm tired of them motherfuckers making us feel less than or making us feel that we have to change things to their fucking standards. Keep your braids. Go in that meeting tomorrow and let them motherfuckers know that you can handle your business and your damn hair and skin color has nothing to do with it!" Charity was sick of the bullshit.

"You're right friend. I'm just tired of the bullshit. We can make good grades in college but still not good enough at work. Black boys can't walk to the damn store with a hoody on. The shit is getting exhausting," Janae felt defeated.

Charity was quiet. Janae was right. They talked a little longer before hanging up. Charity went to the kitchen and decided to make herself a salad for dinner. Her thoughts were consumed with everything going on. Why the hell did the color of her skin matter so much? She was eating her salad, lost in her thoughts when her phone rung. She smiled when Ashton's name popped up.

"What are you up to lady?" Ashton asked her.

"Eating a salad," Charity reported to him.

"Oh really? I'd just ordered some Chinese and was hoping I can come share it with you," Ashton informed her.

"Bring it on. How I'm feeling I can eat everything."

"You ok?" Ashton asked.

"Yea. Will tell you about it when you come," Charity told him.

It wasn't long before he came with the food. It was the first time he came in her house. She'd felt so comfortable with him for some reason.

"Nice place," he told her.

"Thank you," she said leading him to the kitchen.

"This nice ass kitchen but I bet you don't cook," Ashton laughed.

"I do cook. But it's just me and I get tired of cooking small meals."

"I understand. Now you can cook for me."

Charity laughed. He handed her a bottle of wine. "Thought you'd need this after how you sounded on the phone."

"Thank you. I actually do," Charity said.

She took the wine and set it on the bar counter. Pointing to the bar chairs, Ashton took a seat. Charity grabbed some paper plates to put their food on. Opening the cabinet, she grabbed two wine glasses so they could drink some wine.

Over dinner, she told him about Janae and what was going on at her job. She also told him more about her job. He listened attentively as they ate only speaking a few words. It was obvious to him that she needed to vent, and he allowed her to do so. He spoke when he felt she was done.

"That's a lot," Ashton started off. "Sadly, it isn't nothing new. I couldn't get anywhere where I was at, so I started my own firm. It's the only way that I feel I can make a name for myself. There are always a few black faces in top positions, but the truth is they are there for show and the pay still isn't equal to what a white person would get in that same position."

"The shit wrong," Charity said. "Black people have to run when white people can walk slow, and they will get to the same place. The white person would get there faster."

Ashton saw the emotion in Charity's face. He knew she felt every word that she said. For some reason, it made him like her more. She was so passionate and beautiful. She was so right too.

"We got to change the narrative. One person at a time," Ashton said.

"How?" Charity asked.

"Continue to work hard but stand up for what we believe in. Your friend was going to take her braids out. I'm so glad you talked her out of it. Yea she could have done it but what if she wants another hairstyle? Is she going to have to think about what her job would want before every hairstyle? That's not living." Ashton meant every word he said too.

"You are so right," Charity said.

They got quiet and ended up staring at each other. The attraction was real. Ashton leaned in to kiss her and she happily kissed him back. Smiling at each other like teenagers after kissing, they finished their meals then took their wine bottle and wine glasses to the living room in front of the TV. They sipped and talked and basically told each other their life stories. It wasn't long before they both were passed out cuddling on the sofa. It had been a while since Charity slept with a warm body next to her. Though all they'd done was kiss and tickle each other, she liked how it felt. The thought of having a partner to vent to and

lay with at the end of long days was starting to look good.

<u>Chapter 7</u>

Ashton woke up before Charity the next morning. He woke her up. She sat up looking around like she was dreaming until she realized that they'd fallen asleep on the sofa.

"Hey sleepy head," Ashton told her.

"Hey," she smiled.

"Guess we had too much fun last night. I'm going to head home and get dressed for work. Talk to you later," Ashton said. He flashed that perfect white smile.

"Ok," Charity said. "Have a great day." As if on instinct, she leaned in and kissed him on the lips.

"I could get used to those lips," he told her then looked at her lovingly. Then, he glanced at his watch and ran out of the door.

Charity smiled as she stared at the door after he left. Finally, she got up and showered. Throwing on a robe, she fixed a cup of coffee. Looking at the time, she had over an hour before she had to be to work, she used this quiet time to pray and meditate. She prayed for a good day. Ever since Mr. Peter's latest stunt at work, she'd lost some of her motivation. Work was becoming a drag for her.

After getting dressed, she made her way towards work. Getting out of her car, she heard her text notification beep. It was a text from Ashton.

"Stop in on your way in I have something for you."

Charity looked at her watch. She had an extra few minutes, so she rode the elevator to Ashton's floor. She'd never been inside his office before. Walking down the hall, she saw the one with a door with his name on it. It made her smile. She knocked before walking in.

"Come in," he informed her.

In his office was a reception area and waiting room but there was no receptionist. He led her to his office which was around a corner. She loved his big cherry wood desk. He had his degrees hung up behind it.

"I like your place," she let him know.

"It's plain. I'm in the process of decorating and interviewing receptionists. I've been so busy that I've just been locking up every time I leave and answering phones myself." These are for you. He handed her a bag.

"It's a bagel and some hash browns. I got you a black coffee too," he pointed to the coffee on his desk. I put cream and sugar in the bag for you."

"Look at you. This was so thoughtful," Charity smiled and kissed his lips.

"It's the least I could do after falling asleep and spending the night at your house."

"I actually enjoyed sleeping next to you. Even if we were just cramped up on the couch," she admitted to him.

He smiled big. "I did too."

They stared at each other. It was obvious that they were digging each other.

"Well, let me head downstairs. The big case that I worked on will be over today. Mr. Peters would find out if we won or lost."

"With your research, I'm sure he'll win. Have a good day. I'll call you when I leave the courthouse later."

"Sounds good," Charity said smiling then she rode the elevator down to her office.

Once she settled in and turned on her computers and logged into everything, she added a couple of creamers and sugars to her coffee. She ate her bagel and sipped on her coffee throughout the day. She was feeling good, and she knew it had to do with Ashton. It was as if she was in "la la" land. That ended quickly when Mr. Peters walked into her office abruptly.

"Meeting in my office now," he said. His tone wasn't good.

"Ok," Charity said. She was surprised by his tone. He closed the door. She got up wondering what this was all about.

As she walked into his office, she saw Mr. Peters, Katie and Laura Reed. Laura was firm administrator. She handled everything from human resources, mediation, suspensions, promotions, and other things for all the partners of the firm. Seeing her made Charity kind of nervous.

"Hi," Charity told everyone and took a seat.

"We lost the case today Charity. Hundreds of thousands of dollars in retainer fees if we'd won. I thought you had everything laid out. I thought you had the proof in your notes that the plaintiff's injury from years ago wasn't related to the accident." Mr. Peters spoke without explaining what was going on. "This has to go in your file. This was a big mistake. It cost a lot of money. It may even cost us employees because we were counting on that money."

Charity couldn't believe her ears. Was he blaming her for losing the case? "With all due respect Mr. Peters, I went over everything with you. I was supposed to be in the courtroom next to you so that I could help you with anything you forgot. Then when we were to have our final meeting before court started, you had me go over everything with Katie and she hasn't officially become certified yet. I did as I was told. Nothing should be my fault."

Though she was nervous, Charity spoke up for herself. She didn't want anything in her file that she didn't deserve. She worked hard and did her research. Some nights she barely slept. She came home and worked. She loved it but she worked extra hard because she felt like this her personal case since the original plan was for her to sit next to him. She was supposed to be there to remind him of any important factors that he forgot.

Mr. Peters looked at Charity. "There are no excuses for this. We have to write you up."

She looked at him then Laura then Katie. Katie looked like a deer in headlights. She had a nervous stupid look on her face. *Dumb ass blonde*, Charity thought to herself.

"Mr. Peters, I didn't do anything wrong. I did everything ask. Why am I getting written up because you lost your case? Katie was supposed to be there to help with missed stuff so why am I getting punished?"

"Don't speak on anyone else," Mr. Peters told Charity. This was the first time she'd seen him like this.

Laura spoke up, "Look. Everyone calm down. This case was a big loss and we counted on winning. But let's not blame anyone. Let's just take a day or two to calm down."

Mr. Peters didn't say anything. He still looked upset.

"Fine," Mr. Peters told Charity. "I won't write you up, but this is why you don't get to go to court."

Furious but calm Charity asked, "What is why I don't get to go to court? Why did Katie get to go anyway? Is it because she is white? Is my face too dark for court?"

Mr. Peters, Katie, and Laura had a surprised look on their faces. Katie twiddled her thumbs as her face turned red as can be. Laura's eyes widening showed the shock on her face.

"Are you accusing me of being racist?" Mr. Peters asked. He'd stood up. The look on his face showed his irritation. He glared at her with contempt.

Charity suddenly lost her nerve. She definitely was accusing him of being racist. There was no other explanation to want the receptionist in court when she'd been the one who worked vigorously on the case. This was the only case he'd ever lost since she started working there and she'd like to give herself credit for helping with the cases. She took her job serious.

Though all these thoughts crossed her mind, she thought about losing her job. She chose to sit quiet and not say anything else.

Sternly, Laura demanded, "Look, as I stated earlier, we need to take a day or two. Katie get back up front. Stick to up front until you're actually finished with your schooling. We need everyone to have the right accreditations before delving in law and research. Charity take the next couple of days off. Then I'll call you to meet about some things."

Meet about what? Why the fuck am I having to take days off? Charity thought these things to herself but didn't say anything. She just nodded her head and got up. Going to her office, she grabbed her purse out of the drawer and put her cell phone and charger in it. She turned everything off including her lights and shut her office door. She didn't even look at Katie's ass as she left out of the office.

Once in the elevator, she wanted to go to Ashton's office but remembered that he had court. She rode the elevator down and hurriedly marched to her car in the parking garage. Once inside, tears of disappointment fell down her distraught face. *What the hell was going on? Was her hard work being thrown away because Mr. Peters wanted a dumb white face in court instead of her?*

Chapter 8

Janae walked into work dressed to impress. She wore a two-piece pants suit that was black, and her shirt was mixed with black and brown tones. She wore black heels. Her braids were tied neatly back into a bun. She looked very corporate and professional. She was ready to pitch her ad. There was a lot riding on it, and she planned to come out winning. Patricia showed her who she really was, but she was going to show that nothing affected her work ethic.

As Janae walked into the office, things immediately felt strange. The receptionist didn't make eye contact with her. She passed a couple of employees and they were staring but turned away when she looked at them. *What the hell is going on with them?* Janae thought this to herself. She went to her office area that she shared with Patricia. No one was there. The meeting wasn't for a couple of hours so she was sure Patricia would be in soon.

Janae hadn't gotten much sleep last night. She went over everything so that it would be perfect. She also couldn't get Patricia's words out of her mind. Did she actually think the clients wouldn't want to do business because it was a black woman's idea? That was ridiculous. It was 2019 after all. It was obvious to her that Patricia felt some type of way about black people. Hopefully, she would get the promotion and they wouldn't have to work side by side anymore. It was going to be awkward. Janae almost took out her braids last night. But she couldn't in the end because she refused to change her hairstyle to fit Patricia or any other white person.

A couple of hours passed, and it was time for the meeting. Patricia still hadn't arrived. Just when Janae got worried, Patricia walked in the office.

"There you are. Where were you? I was getting worried that you would miss the meeting," Janae sputtered.

Patricia wasn't giving Janae any eye contact. Things felt weird. She hung up her coat and put her briefcase on her desk then she finally turned around towards Janae. There was a nervous look in her eyes and Janae's heart sunk. She knew some bullshit was going on.

"Everything ok?" Janae questioned.

Patricia gave a nervous smile. "Actually, everything is great. I have some stupendous news."

Janae felt relieved. "Ok. What is it?"

"Well, the clients called last night and asked about doing the meeting earlier. I didn't want to bother you, so I gave them the quick pitch, but I gave you your credit. We got the account and I'm giving you the whole bonus."

Janae was stunned. She didn't know how to feel. Of course, the bonus was part of her goal, but she also wanted to pitch her own idea.

"Why didn't you tell me?" Janae asked Patricia. "You know how much I wanted to pitch my own idea. I was up all night and up early getting ready."

Patricia felt grody. "I'm so sorry Janae. They know it was your idea. I didn't take your credit. It was a great idea and they loved it."

"Why didn't you just tell me so that I could be there myself? I don't understand," Janae exclaimed. She was furious but mostly hurt because she knew why Patricia didn't tell her. All this time she'd worked under Patricia, she didn't have a clue how she felt about black people. Now she knew. She couldn't pitch her own idea she'd worked months perfecting all because of a damn hairstyle.

"I just wanted to make sure we get the account. It was nothing personal. I don't want the money. You still get the credit," Patricia assured her.

"So, you didn't think we could get the account with me there? Because of my braids? It's just a hairstyle,"

Janae couldn't believe what she was hearing. And she kept mentioning the bonus money like that would make Janae feel better. It wasn't just about money for her. This was her entire idea and she wanted to present it herself.

"No. It's just that I wasn't sure how the clients would think. They're rich and seem to prefer certain things," Patricia was trying to explain.

"So rich clients don't prefer blacks?"

"It's not that. I just wish you'd worn your normal long hair. That way they would know you were different. Braids seem hoodlum to some people even though it's wrong," Patricia told me.

Janae couldn't believe what she was hearing but she remained calm. "So, I look hoodlum?"

"No. I'm not saying that. Look I'm explaining it all wrong. You are wonderful and educated and I know your capabilities. Sometimes these prestigious people draw conclusions based on simple things, like braids. I don't like it, but I really wanted the account for us. I handled it all wrong. I'm so sorry."

Janae was quiet. There were so many things she wanted to say to Patricia. She wanted to tell her that the dumb blonde stigma really did apply to her sometimes. She wanted to ask her how she even got the position because she didn't know anything. The ideas of those who worked with her saved her ass most of the time.

Patricia continued, "Just think. You get bonus. It looks good when time for a promotion. And the client knows your name and that it's your idea. You'll meet soon."

"Didn't they ask where I was? They didn't want to know why I wasn't there?" Janae asked.

"I told them you were sick. I'm so sorry," Patricia said. "But you're a genius. Everyone knows you're great at what you do." She smiled hoping things were all better now.

Janae gave a fake smirk looking smile. There was so much more she wanted to say but it was no use. What could she do now? Patricia knew exactly what she was doing.

"You know what? As a reward for working hard, take the rest of the day off. Tomorrow is Friday so take that off too. With pay! And you won't have to use your personal time. You deserve it. Hell, I'm going to take tomorrow off too. When we get back Monday, we will get started on the new project! I'll go over everything from the meeting then," Patricia sounded excited. She truly thought she was doing Janae a favor by giving her a couple of days off.

Janae felt so exasperated and defeated that she faked a smile and said, "Ok. Taking a couple of days off actually sounds good right now. I could use a drink."

Patricia smiled. "That's right. Get a drink. Celebrate your achievements!"

Janae grabbed her things and fake smiled again. "Ok. See you Monday. Call me if you need me."

Patricia smiled. "Ok. Enjoy."

Janae walked out. The receptionist bitch still wasn't looking at her. Did everyone know what Patricia did? Did everyone know she wasn't included in the meeting for her own damn idea?

Chapter 9

Charity's phone rung. She didn't want to answer. She was home watching Netflix upset about what happened at work. Looking at the caller ID, she saw that it was Janae.

"Hey girl," Janae said sounding down.

"What's wrong? You're feeling like I'm feeling. I was just sent home from work cause of some shit that white receptionist bitch did!" Charity told her friend.

"What the hell? Some bullshit going on at work with me too. I'm on the way. Want me to bring anything?"

"I got enough liquor in wine in my lil bar. Bring some food I ain't ate shit and it's past lunchtime."

"Cool, I'm hungry too," Janae said.

It was less than 30 minutes later when Janae arrived. She'd went to Charity's favorite sub place and bought a family sub that was cut up smaller sandwiches. In addition to the sandwiches, they had chips and pickles.

"That look good as hell. I didn't realize how hungry I was," Charity told her best friend.

They started eating and Charity told Janae about possibly being written up for leaving out pertinent case information when Katie'd taken over the case and she told her everything as instructed.

"That's some fuck shit," Janae said. "I always wanted to believe that things were better in our world than the things our grandparents and great-grandparents had to put up with. I knew we had to play the part to a certain extent like be professional, work hard so they can't say we're slackers, the normal stuff that every one of every color should have to do. But, we can't wear our hair how we want? That is crazy. "

"It is fucking crazy, and Patricia is wrong," Charity said.

They spent most of the day talking about all the injustices that blacks must endure. Some black people thought that those working in the corporate world had it good and they'd "made it" but the truth was they were expected to kiss ass, work triple everyone else and shut the fuck up and not complain about anything.

After several hours, Ashton called. Charity was tipsy from all the wine they'd been drinking. She slurred while talking to him.

"Hey bae," Charity dragged out.

He thought it was cute. "Sounds like someone is feeling good."

"Yea. In here drinking and drowning our sorrows," Charity muttered sounding sad.

"Why? What's wrong baby?" The sound of concern in his voice was sweet.

Charity told him what was going on with her and Janae's situation. Imagine how upset he was when she told him the whole shebang.

"It is illegal what your boss is trying to do," the lawyer side of him came out strong.

He sympathized with them because he knew exactly how they felt. In law school, he'd been discriminated against by certain professors. It hurt his feelings, but he worked hard and made the best grades. He interned at a prestigious law firm and did a great job but even there he could feel the indifferences. Briefly after graduating, he worked there to pay bills and figure things out. Once he'd built a few clients and won some good cases, he'd made the decision to open his own firm. He knew it wouldn't be easy, but he vowed to make it work.

Ashton stopped by Charity's house and bought dinner for her and Janae. She'd mentioned one time that she loved seafood, so he bought fried shrimp, fried fish and French fries.

"He's a keeper," Janae told Charity then turned to Ashton. "Her drunk behind is being rude so I'll introduce myself. I'm Janae her best friend but we're more like sisters. I don't play about her so honesty is everything."

Ashton laughed, he thought it was cute that Charity had a best friend. Studying and working hard kept him from having many friends and lots of guys that he'd grown up with were unfortunately in jail or content with living as they always did. They didn't want more out of life. Since he'd been a kid, he saw his mom work hard to provide for him and his sister. He'd always wanted to be able to take the load off of her. He was a lawyer, and his sister was a registered nurse. His mom did well. She lived in a nice condo that she owned on the outskirts of their hometown up in Connecticut. After finishing college in Atlanta, Georgia, Ashton decided to stay there. His sister wasn't too far in Columbia, South Carolina. There wasn't much snow in the South and he really enjoyed that.

"Nice to meet you Janae," Ashton finally said after smirking. "I'm an honest person."

"No, you're not, you're a lawyer," Janae told him.

Ashton laughed, "Ok. You got me. But I am honest when it comes to my personal life. Sometimes in business you have to fib to get your way."

"Don't pay her any attention," Charity told him. "She's the biggest "fibber" in the world."

Ashton laughed again. Charity got up to get paper plates so that they could enjoy the food he'd bought over.

"Would you like me to put everything in the kitchen?" he asked Charity.

"No. Today we're feeling sorry for ourselves so we're going to be sloppy and eat in the living room. As long as we clean up after ourselves," Charity gazed at Janae.

Janae cut her eyes and they fixed their plates. Charity continued to share more details with Ashton about what happened at work with her and at work with Janae.

"That's really messed up," Ashton acknowledged, "starting with your job, your boss has lost his mind. He can't legally reprimand you. Everything falls on Katie but it's really not her fault either. She was thrown in at the end and you were thrown off in the end. The fault lies solely on Mr. Peters. I can represent you against them. Do not sign that write-up," Ashton demanded.

Charity sighed, "If I got a lawyer, they'd really be mad and treat me differently. It's already awkward not being able to do what the other paralegals are allowed to do by other partners."

Ashton went into lawyer mode. "You can't say what goes on with the other partners in the company, but we clearly see Mr. Peters is biased against you. You've been doing a great job yet haven't gotten privileges as other counterparts in your same job position. He took a damn receptionist and gave her your job to do then blamed you for it not turning out well. I'm also willing to bet that if we subpoena the company's payroll, you are being paid less than the others in your position. We all know this is race-related too."

Charity was quiet. He was talking so fast that she couldn't keep up. She didn't know what to do.

"Right now, I don't know what I want to do. I have a LOT to think about over these next few days," Charity admitted. She knew how they were treating her was wrong, but she didn't know if she should let them know how she really felt. It could cause her to lose her job.

"Yea think about it baby," Ashton said. He hadn't meant to call her baby, but it slipped out. He was really digging her.

"Baby?" Janae questioned.

"You catch everything," Charity said, throwing a sofa pillow on her friend.

"What do you think about my situation?" Janae asked him seriously. "I still got credit for the ad and I'm getting the bonus, so they really didn't do anything to me right?"

"Yes, they did!" Ashton said with passion. "You couldn't pitch your own ad to a client because you changed your hairstyle? That's crazy and very racist as hell. Your boss doesn't like your "black" hairstyle and it's obvious. She blamed the client's taste, but the clients have never met you so how would she know their taste?"

Janae and Charity listened to Ashton. His feelings were evident.

"But what can I really do if I'm being paid for it?" Janae asked.

"You can sue for discrimination or you can just let your boss run the shots and determine who can and who can't see your "black" face," Ashton said. "She basically hid you from the client because you're black and embracing a hairstyle worn by your culture."

"Damn," Janae said. "I was feeling some type of way but couldn't think exactly what was wrong since I got my bonus, but you summed it up. That bitch basically hid me from our clients because SHE didn't like my braids."

"That is fucked up," Charity interjected. She only cussed when she was drinking or upset and at this point, she was both. "We work hard and do basic things because our skin is black, or they don't like our hairstyle? It's crazy. Yet a receptionist bitch who is studying for my job and not even finished with school yet can do things that I can't even do in my job position. Shit is crazy as hell. There is no other reason except she is white. Unless he's fucking her!"

Ashton laughed at Charity. She was right. On any given day, black people went through fuck shit at work while white people were given chances and excuses for the things, they did wrong.

They talked some more about what possible cases they had against their jobs. Charity was glad that she had Ashton in her life to discuss these types of things with. It saddened her that so many people in lower positions than them dealt with this and there seemed to be nothing they could do but deal with it or lose their job.

Chapter 10

The next day was Friday and Charity decided to deep clean her house since she was off from work. She'd woken up and spoken to Ashton on his way to work. He would be busy until later which was good because Charity needed time to herself to think about some things. The steps she took next needed to be hers and not steps taken because of anyone else. The thought of going to work made her want to throw up. How could Mr. Peters treat her like that after everything she'd done. Sleep was foreign when she worked on cases for him because she didn't want to miss anything. And to think he wanted her to get in trouble because he didn't do his job? It really pissed her off. It made her more upset knowing that if she were white none of this would have happened.

Once her house was clean, she ordered some food to be delivered. She didn't want to put on clothes and go anywhere. Soap Operas were on TV. She hadn't watched them since she was a child with her grandmother. It was funny to see some of the same characters on there. They were just older. Bored with soaps, she decided to do what she did best. Research. She decided to research laws regarding race and workplace discrimination.

Hours had passed and she'd looked into a lot of information. There was a place called the EEOC which stood for Equal Employment Opportunity Commission. It was a government place that research claims of job discrimination. The law stated that jobs couldn't discriminate against you for the color of your skin, for having a disability, for your age, gender or retaliation. There'd been many cases that were won by the employees. One of the cases won involved black employees finding out white people in same positions made double their pay rate. The black employees did a class action suit and won big. Another case involved the human resource manager being friends with an Accounting manager. Because of this, employee complaints about the manager discriminating against black workers, would go unnoticed. The person complaining would actually get into trouble. Finally, an employee was smart enough to document conversations by email and got enough proof to win a lawsuit. She took notes of any important information she'd learned about workplace bias.

Looking at the time, she decided to call and check on Janae. She'd researched some things about her situation as well. It was clear to her that they both had a case. But, in creating a case, there were things to worry about. Work would be even more awkward. Big cases and important job duties may be taken away. And if they didn't win, they could be fired or feel humiliated. The main thing for her was being able to pay bills without the job. She did have a savings.

Janae didn't answer so she decided to put her research away. Looking at the time, she knew Ashton would be off soon. Wanting to call him, she decided against it. She didn't want to appear needy though she was really digging him. It had been a while since a man had been so attentive to her. She liked it. The fact that they had working in law in common made things even better for her. As if he knew he was on her mind, he sent her a text.

Good evening beautiful. I'd like to take your mind off of your troubles and take you to dinner and maybe a movie? Feel up to it?

Charity smiled so hard looking at the text. She could feel butterflies in her stomach. Thinking of Ashton made her feel free. It was really feeling like this man could be the one for her. During this time, she should be really upset about what was going on at work and though she was, this new man in her life was making her happy. She responded to his text.

Yes, I feel up to it. Tell me the time and I'll be ready

She loved putting emojis with her text messages to him. Her smile was like that of the smiley face that she sent. She headed to her bedroom to find a cute outfit to wear on her date.

~

Janae was home basically having the same kind of day as Charity. She'd chosen to spend the day thinking about how she wanted to handle things. The lawyer point-of-view information from Ashton sounded good but unlike Charity, she didn't have a nice savings if things went wrong. The bonus would help but would she get it if she sued them for racial discrimination. This was the best paying job she'd ever had. *Should she risk losing it for a hairstyle? Maybe she could conform to what they want just to make money.*

Just as soon as she thought it, she knew it wasn't her. She wasn't going to be comfortable in that work environment after what happened. Maybe she could just ask to meet the clients. It's not like she hadn't expressed how she felt. There was really nothing to do about it now since the meeting had already happened. All types of crazy thoughts went through her head. The sound of the phone ringing took her out of her trance.

It was Patricia calling from work. Why was she calling when she told her to enjoy a few days off? Janae didn't want to answer the phone, but she did anyway.

"Hello?"

"Hey. I don't mean to disturb you. I just wanted you to know your bonus check will be here Monday," Patricia said.

"Wow. That's fast. Ok."

"Aren't you going to ask how much?" Patricia asked. It was as if she was anxious for her to know.

"No. I have an idea, but I'll see when it comes." Janae secretly wanted to know but she was not thirsty and would never allow herself to seem thirsty to anyone.

Besides, amounts had been thrown out in the past, so she had an idea.

"Well ok. You'll see anyway. I emailed you some forms to read and sign. Once they're filled out and emailed back to me, I'll make sure you check is ready. Take your time. Email by Sunday night if you can so I can get the check approved to go into your account on Monday."

"Ok. Sounds good," Janae replied. She just wanted to get off the phone.

"Ok. And sorry for interrupting your free time," Patricia said before hanging up.

The call was very weird to Janae. She'd gotten bonuses before and never had to sign papers. Her bonuses in the past had been along the lines of $500-$800 which was a lot of extra money in her eyes. But it was rumored that this bonus would be along the lines of $3000 since it was her idea. Additionally, there was a pay raise since she would oversee the project. She reckoned that all those details were in the agreement coming in the email. Wanting to not think more about the job, Janae decided to check the email later. *Them motherfuckers were being slick trying to give her the bonus so quick anyway.*

<u>Chapter 11</u>

Charity had a great night with Ashton. They'd eaten Italian food at a great restaurant. He'd ordered them an expensive bottle of wine and Charity felt special. Deciding to talk about anything but work, she'd told him her life story. He said he wanted to meet her mother and would take her the next time she visited. Charity laughed. Her family always felt she worked too hard for men, but they didn't understand that there were men who worked just as hard.

They went to the movies after the restaurant. Maybe they should have gone before dinner because Charity's ass fell asleep in the movie. Ashton laughed and let her sleep. When she woke up it was nearing the end. It was a black love comedy that she suggested, and she had the nerve to fall asleep.

"What's going on?" Charity opened her eyes. She'd been lying on Ashton's chest in the movies.

"Your ass fell asleep that's what's going on. Too much wine," he laughed.

"Damn I wanted to see this movie," she fake pouted.

Ashton kissed her on the lips. They looked into each other's eyes and it was as if Charity felt a spark. She was digging this guy.

"Let's go sleepy-head," Ashton told her. She laughed and they got up and left the movies.

Pulling up to Charity's house, Ashton turned the car off but didn't take the keys out.

"I enjoyed myself," he gushed.

"I enjoyed myself too. I'm usually home working or just watching Netflix on a Friday night. It feels good to have someone to do things with," Charity admitted.

They kissed passionately. Charity was moist. It had been over a year since she'd had sex.

"Well, I'll walk you to the door before leaving," Ashton promised.

Looking into his eyes she asked, "do you have to leave?"

Nothing else was said. They got out of the car. She had her keys in one hand and Ashton held her other hand. Quickly, she opened the door, and they went in. After locking it, she dropped her purse on the table and turned around to face Ashton. They kissed passionately. It felt like magic. They continued kissing and her juices moistened. Taking his hand, she led him to the bedroom. Slowly, they undressed each other. Laying her down on the bed, Ashton kissed her all over. He slowly stuck his penis in her and was surprised about how moist it was. That night, they made slow passionate love all night.

~

The next morning Charity woke up first. It was after 8am. She went to use her bathroom and brush her teeth.

Heading back towards the bed, he looked to be sleeping so peacefully. Last night had been special for them both. Their bodies were in sync. Charity really enjoyed it. Thinking about it made her decide to cook him breakfast. She knew he planned on going into the office later so he may as well eat first.

Looking in her refrigerator, she had some eggs, and she had some bacon. Searching her cabinet for grits, she was unsuccessful so settled for biscuits. She'd whipped them up some eggs, bacon and biscuits. She'd also made some coffee because she was tired. Going back into the room with their food, Ashton was moving around. She blushed as she noticed his hand searching the bed for her.

"I'm right here," she said.

He smiled. "Oh, you got up early since you slept in the movies."

Charity laughed. "I really woke up to pee. And I decided to cook breakfast, so you won't say I starved you the first night that you spent the night."

"I appreciate it. We worked off that dinner last night."

Charity blushed and they kissed. After eating breakfast, they laid around and ended up having sex again. When they were done Ashton said, "I wanna lay in bed with you all day but I gotta go."

"I know you gotta work baby," Charity said.

"What are you doing today?" Ashton asked her.

"Nothing much. I may go to Janae's house since I couldn't reach her yesterday."

"Sounds good," Ashton said. He threw on his clothes. "I'm going to run home and get washed up then head to the office and finish some loose ends. Can I see you tonight beautiful?"

"Of course," she told him while blushing.

Tired, she took a nap when he left. Waking up a couple of hours later, she showered and got dressed. Instead of calling Janae, she decided to pop up to her house to see what she was up to.

It wasn't long before she pulled up and knocked on her friend's door. Janae answered with some cute pajamas on.

"So, we're popping up and not calling?" she said as she let Charity in.

"You didn't answer or call me yesterday, so I wanted to check on you."

"I'm good. Patrice's ass called. They're giving me the bonus Monday already. It's like her ass knows she's wrong as hell," Janae said.

"Monday? Damn, that is quick. I thought it took weeks to get a bonus for accounts y'all land."

"I know," Janae shook her head. She grabbed her laptop and decided to find the email and look over the contract and bonus amount. "Let me see what this contract says. I didn't even read the shit yet. I was relaxing and didn't want to deal with work."

"Same here. We went out last night and didn't discuss work. It was wonderful," Charity said.

"Look at you smiling," Janae said. She planned on teasing Charity more. Her eyes were on the contract at this moment though. "What kind of shit is this?"

"What's going on?" Charity asked.

"This contract. They're giving me a bigger bonus than expected. It's $7,000 instead of $3,000 like I thought."

"What? That's good," Charity said. "That kind of bonus makes you wanna overlook the racist shit. You may need to give Patrice one more chance."

"But," Janae continued, "it comes with stipulations. It says by signing the contract and taking the bonus, I can't bring up her not allowing me to meet clients and I have to be ok with taking my braids out and wearing my normal hairstyle.”

“What the fuck? So, she’s saying here’s some extra money bitch, but your black ass needs to take your ghetto ass braids out and don’t mention not meeting our clients again! That’s crazy as hell!”

The look on Janae’s face showed that she was livid. Tears were in her eyes.

“I spent the weekend thinking about everything,” Janae said when she finally spoke. “And even though it’s wrong, I was still going to go to work and not complain. No lawsuit. No nothing. I just was going to continue to work hard and save my money. One day, I will have enough clients to work for myself. I was going to let her racist ass have her way while I stack my money.”

Charity was quiet as her friend talked.

“But this bitch had the NERVE to tell me to take my braids out as part of getting MY bonus for MY damn ad! I'm done now!" Tears flowed from Janae's eyes. "It's 2020 and we're still dealing with fuck shit! I got a degree. My dumb ass purposely wore my hair like I thought they'd like for a long time. I did everything that I thought I should do to be successful. But I can't wear braids when the fuck I want? Hell no! I'm not signing that shit!"

"I don't blame you friend. Her dumb ass basically incriminated herself with that contract. She just thought that fat ass bonus would shut your black ass up!" Charity spoke. The shit pissed her off. Why was it so hard being black? Why was the color of their skin looked at as wrong?

"Yea. Like I said at first I was going to ignore it but tell Ashton I'd like to make an appointment with him Monday if possible."

"Ok. But what are you going to do in the meantime? She wants it signed by Sunday, so she knows what she was doing. Are you going to tell her Monday that you won't sign?" Charity asked her friend.

"Yes. I'm going to tell her Monday I won't sign. I'll let Ashton tell me how I should handle everything else," Janae said.

"Sounds good. I was reading about the EEOC and a lot of shit today."

"Oh yea Mrs. Paralegal. Have you decided how to handle your job?"

"I'm not signing shit because I didn't do shit wrong. I plan to work as usual. Not sure how that will go but we'll see. It's time to stand up for ourselves. So many other black people in good jobs like ours are scared to stand up for what's right because they want to continue making money to pay their bills," Charity said. "Them fuckers know that too that's why they treat us like shit."

"Right!" Janae chimed in.

It was clear that she was still pissed but Charity saw the hurt on her friend's face. She really loved her job and she thought Patricia was different. It hurt her to know that

Patricia was just like the rest of them. She just knew how to play her part right. That's why she was so successful. Well, she was going to learn that Janae knew how to play her part too.

Chapter 12

It was Monday and Charity dreaded getting up for work. She'd spent most of Sunday with Ashton, but he didn't spend the night. They both needed rest for the week ahead and they both knew they wouldn't sleep much if he spent the night. Charity pulled herself together and washed up and got dressed. She made sure she looked professional and cute. She knew she would see Ashton during the workday.

Once she arrived at work, she walked in her office and started turning everything on. She'd stopped to grab some coffee and a breakfast sandwich on the way in. Ashton had to handle some things to the courthouse and wouldn't be back for a couple of hours that's why she didn't get him any. There was some work she needed to catch up on and she was happy about it. Her plan was to just keep busy all day. Hopefully, the weekend would have given Mr. Peters time to think, and he would realize trying to write her up for something she didn't do was wrong.

Charity was so absorbed into her work that she didn't notice how late it had gotten. Glancing at her clock, it was 11:00. It was surprising Mr. Peters hadn't come to her office yet. Needing to use the restroom, she got up and walked past the lobby to go out to where the restrooms were. Katie was at the front desk now. She hadn't been in yet when Charity had gotten to work earlier. To make things amicable, Charity didn't even look her way.

Charity wondered if Ashton'd gotten back from court yet. She started to go down to his office but decided against it. It was almost lunch time so she decided she may as well wait. Walking back in the office, Katie looked at her nervously.

"Hi," Katie told her.

"Hey," Charity mumbled and quickly walked back into her office.

Sitting back at her desk, she noticed some new emails. She clicked on the one that was from Laura Reed, the firm administrator. There was a meeting request attached to the email. It was scheduled for 2:00 that day. Charity sighed. Now I gotta spend lunch break wondering what she wants. I will not sign a write-up. She thought all these thoughts to herself. The nervousness she was feeling didn't sit well with her. Why should she be dealing with this? She'd gone over everything with Katie as instructed. After undergoing sleepless nights for that research, she should be the one lodging a complaint. His ass was the one who needed to be written up. Is this meeting the reason he hasn't gotten to work yet?

After spending minutes sitting in a daze, she got a text that made her smile.

I'm back from court and bought us some subs and chips for lunch. Are you able to take a   lunch today?

Yes, I'm able and I'm coming now! Charity texted back so fast. She was relieved that he was back, and she would be able to talk with him before her stupid meeting.

She snatched up her purse so fast and speed walked out of her office. Walking out, she kept looking straight. There was no way she wanted to look at Katie's ass right now. It was weird how she felt Katie's eyes staring at the back of her. She'd almost made it to the door when she heard her voice.

"Hey Charity," she heard Katie say.

"Hey," Charity said, turning around. Her face made it apparent that she was in a rush.

"I know you gotta go but I just want to say I'm sorry about the other day. I told him it was my fault not yours," Katie had a sorry look on her face.

"Ok thank you," Charity said, as she quickly turned back around to walk away.

It was apparent that Katie wanted to talk more but Charity wasn't in the mood. Her apology was appreciated though. At least someone acknowledged the truth in the situation. Relief was felt when she finally reached the elevators. Getting on, she pressed the button to the 3rd floor. It didn't take her long to reach Ashton's office at all. She knocked then walked in when she noticed it was open.

"Hey baby," Ashton said. "I wasn't expecting you to take lunch as soon as I texted but I'm happy to see you."

He shut his office door but didn't lock it. He led her to his conference room area. They could see if a client or someone walked in from there. She plopped in a chair looking exasperated. He handed her a water bottle from the refrigerator then started pulling their food out of the bag.

"Is everything ok baby?" he asked. He figured some stuff would happen at work today.

"Yea," she sighed. "Mr. Peters isn't in the office today. I'm glad but then I got a meeting later with our firm administrator. I know it's about the write-up stuff. I'm not signing it. On the way here, Katie stopped me and admitted it was her fault. I gave her all the information needed for the case. Not to mention, he usually goes over everything with me continuously but chose not to. He wanted Katie to do it."

"I hate you're dealing with this baby. Don't sign the paper. I can come down with you as your lawyer," he suggested.

"No. It's just a meeting. I will handle myself accordingly and I ain't signing shit."

"Good. Now let's eat," Ashton said.

As they ate, he told her about his day in court. He also complimented her outfit and expressed to her how pretty she was. He knew how to lay it on. She was so comfortable with him. In the wake of having big issues, she still wasn't stressed because she was happy to have him in her life.

"There's another thing I've been meaning to talk with you about."

"What is it?" she asked him. It made her nervous when certain people wanted to "talk."

"I want you to come work for me. Well with me," he told her.

"Really?" she asked. "We're just getting to know each other. That probably won't be a good idea. And what if we don't work out? Then I'll be out of a job for real."

"No, you wouldn't be out of a job. I promise," Ashton told her. "Think about it is all that I'm saying. I need help. You can help me with some research and be office manager and help me find a receptionist to hire. If we're not busy, you can work less and study for school when you. We can create a contract to both our liking and in it I will put that if our friendship doesn't work out, you will still have your job. If you don't want it, you have to give me 3 months' notice to find someone else."

Charity stared at him. "Well dang. You thought of everything didn't you?"

"I did," he admitted. "I enjoy getting to know you and I hope it leads into something beautiful. But even if you decide you hate me and don't want me to ever be your man, I don't want to lose a good potential employee. You're smart as hell. You work hard. You care about your job and the law. It would be crazy for me to hire anyone other than you."

Charity was quiet. It sounded good but it sounded too good. What if whatever they were doing didn't lead to anything? Would they still be able to be friends and work together? It would be taking a big chance leaving her position. But her job was getting crazy and uncomfortable.

"That's a lot to think about baby. But I really appreciate you for thinking of me. Give me a couple of weeks before I say yes or no. Ok?"

"Take as much time as you need," he flashed that smile that she liked so much. "I just need you to know you have options. And I really need help. You don't have to take their bullshit. Just know that." Ashton looked so damn fine when he was talking seriously.

Charity stared at him blushing. "You're a pretty good person Mr. Ashton. You lay the charm on thick."

He laughed.

"Well, I really enjoyed lunch. It's hard going back up there to work. I'll talk to you later." Charity got up to leave.

He got up and walked her to the door. He kissed her lips. "Good luck at your meeting."

"Thank you, baby," the smile on Charity's face was bright. Meeting or not meeting. She was happy these days and it was because of Ashton.

Charity got to her desk and was lost in her thoughts. Ashton had given her something to think about. It was crazy how things had gotten so weird at work. Another email popped up. It was from Laura again. Looking at the time, it wasn't quite 2:00 yet so what did Laura's sickening ass won't. She clicked on the email. It was a notification saying the meeting is cancelled and would be rescheduled.

"Ain't this a bitch!" Charity thought.

She hated the waiting game! She just wanted to know what the meeting was about.

Chapter 13

Janae walked into work at her normal time on Monday. She'd gotten upset about the contract this weekend, but she kept her game face on. Her talent was undeniable, and she was definitely an asset to the company. Hopefully, she would be able to get her deserved bonus whether she signed a racist ass contract or not.

Usually, Janae beat Patricia to work so she was surprised to see her already sitting in their office space.

"Good morning," Patricia said.

"Good morning," Janae told her and went to her desk area.

"I came in early to get things started for your bonus, but I didn't see your email with the contract."

"That's because I'm not signing it. Why would you think it would be ok to dictate how I should wear my hair at work? And why would that go in my contract for a bonus that I earned already?" Janae got straight to the point. There was no way to sugarcoat the contract situation.

"We talked about this already. I'm just trying to ensure that my protégé is successful," Patricia told Janae. It was like she just didn't get how fucked up she was making the situation.

"Well, honestly, it's racist. Braids are part of my culture. I shouldn't have to keep wearing my hair a certain way to get a bonus or get "certain" clients. It's racist. We both know it. If you leave me alone about my hair, never stop me from meeting a client again, and give me my bonus without a ridiculous contract then I'm willing to forget all of this happened and we can go back to working great together as usual."

Janae had discussed with Ashton that she wanted to give Patricia a chance to redeem herself. She was hoping maybe she would correct her wrongdoing and no action had to be taken. She didn't want to go against her and the company for racial discrimination. Even though she knew she had a case, she didn't want things to go down bad. It didn't have to. A simple apology and acknowledgment of wrongdoing could go a long way.

Patricia looked at Janae. It was obvious that she was choosing her words carefully. Saying the wrong thing could do more harm and she didn't want that.

"I'm sorry you feel that way Janae. We are not a racist company. Would you be here if we were? There are just certain rules and policies that we want followed. It has to do with professionalism and nothing to do with race." Patricia spoke calm yet matter-of-factly.

"It is racist to tell me to change my hairstyle and never wear it again. This hairstyle is part of my culture. My idea and hard work earned us that client. Sorry you were too ashamed of my black face to let me meet them. Either way, my bonus has already been earned whether I sign the contract or not. I'm not signing it so what's next?" Janae said what needed to be said. It stunned her that it was going this far.

Patricia sighed. "Janae. Why do you want to make things difficult? Just sign the contract and get your big bonus. I know you noticed it's double what you thought."

"Patricia, it insults me that you think adding to my bonus will make me agree to your racist terms. Now are you going to give me my bonus or not?" Janae was done playing games with Patricia. "My bonus has been earned so you're saying you're not giving me what's owed to me?"

"I'll talk with the CFO. Maybe I can get you the original $3000. The other part of the bonus was with those conditions. You're hindering your career by not making a few simple changes. I just wanted to groom you into the best. You used to say you looked up to me. I really like you and feel that I can help you win in this industry! Your color doesn't matter to me. It's everyone else that I feel it matters too!" Patricia rambled on.

"My color doesn't matter to you, but it matters to others? What others?" Janae wanted to know. Did the higher ups tell her to keep my black ass out of everyone's face? She thought this to herself.

"Look. We've worked together awhile. You know I adore you. I promise I want to see you win," Patricia said.

Janae didn't know what else to say. Part of her felt that Patricia's liking for her was real and that maybe her bosses was the reason for her behavior. But if that were true, why wouldn't she stand up to them? Didn't she understand that she was participating in their racist bullshit?

"Look Patricia. I really like you too. But I told you how I feel," Janae said. She was done talking. She'd said what she said.

"I understand. Like I said, I'll arrange your original bonus because you did earn it."

"Thanks," Janae said, not knowing what else to say. "If you don't mind, I'm going to work from home the rest of the day. I have some emails and miscellaneous stuff to catch up on. I'll be available by email or phone."

"That actually sounds good. We won't start working on our new contract until next week anyway. I'm probably going to finish a few things and work from home the rest of the day myself. We deserve it," Patricia smiled trying to lighten the mood.

Janae fake smiled and gathered her files and laptop and put them in her bag. Leaving work, she didn't know what the next step would be. But, she did know that she couldn't let her job get away with their racist bullshit. It was unwarranted and she didn't deserve it at all. And when she thought of people who were in lower positions or who couldn't afford to fight their jobs for racist treatment, it made her want to fight more.

<u>**Chapter 14**</u>

Janae and Ashton were having a meeting at Charity's house. They were discussing the lawsuit that Janae planned on filing against her company. Charity listened in but didn't say anything. It was their business and Ashton meant serious business when he was in lawyer mode. She fried them some hamburgers and French fries. Her and Janae liked to pig out when they were stressed and they both were stressed because of work.

They'd finished up for the most part when the food got ready. She saw Janae sign some papers.

"Y'all hungry?" Charity asked.

"Starving!" Ashton said. He looked at Janae, "So you know the plan?"

"Yes. File claim with the EEOC so it will be on record. Then, go to work. Work hard. Don't mention bonus unless they mention it and stand your ground professionally. When will you serve them? Tomorrow evening?" Janae said.

"I'll try. Sometimes it takes a couple of days. Just don't miss work. They may retaliate against you but that will make our case even stronger."

"Ok," Janae said. "I hate this shit, but it has to be done. It's just going to feel awkward at work now." She sighed.

"I understand," Charity said. "I would have rather gone to the meeting than cancel it. Now I'm wondering what tomorrow has in store." Charity said.

"Well, you know what you can do," Ashton said. He was referring to his offer to Charity. She hadn't told Janae about it yet and didn't want to right now.

She rolled her eyes at him then smiled. They ate their food, and he answered some more questions for Janae. Things were getting real, and it was nerve-wrecking. But it was time to stand up for all the black girls working in a corporate world.

~

The next day Charity walked into work. Katie smiled and spoke, so she did the same. After settling in, she worked on some things that needed to be done. Her plan was to occupy her time until it was time to go. She was so busy at the computer that she didn't notice her office door open. It was Mr. Peters.

"Good afternoon," he told her.

Looking at the clock she didn't realize it was afternoon already. She hadn't eaten lunch yet, but she had a feeling after this conversation that she would be happy to leave the building.

"Good afternoon," she said to him. She tried smiling but it was hard after the stunt he pulled.

"I just wanted to apologize to you about the other day. I was upset after court and blamed you. It wasn't your fault. It was mine. You won't be written up and I am sorry," Mr. Peters told her.

What the hell? Charity thought to herself. What was going on? One day he is angry and wants to write her up. Then the Firm Administrator requested a meeting with her then cancelled it. What was going on that she didn't know about?

"I appreciate your apology," she told him.

"Thank you. And next big case, I PROMISE you'll be right beside me," he told her.

"I would love that," Charity said even though she didn't believe him. This was something he said every time that he knew she was disappointed or upset about something.

He left her office, and she was happy to see him leave. Why did he have a change of heart anyway? Did

Katie talk to him? Something was fishy and the lawyer in her wanted to find out exactly what it was.

~

A few days later, Janae was at work. Ashton made it clear that she should conduct business as usual. It had been a few days, but he wasn't sure how soon the company would be served the court papers but either way she had to do her job as any other day. They would possibly be looking for excuses to fire her after getting the lawsuit papers. The reason most people didn't sue was because of how the tension in the workplace could get afterwards. It would be hard, but Janae vowed to stick with it. She wasn't fighting for just herself; she was fighting for other minorities who couldn't afford to stand up for themselves.

Patricia came in shortly after her, as usual. They said good morning to each other and started on work they had to catch up on. The truth was Patricia didn't know how to interact with Janae now. Their conversations lately had been strictly about work. She didn't want to bring the subject up right now. There was enough work to be done to keep them both busy the rest of the day.

After coming in from lunch, Janae walked back in the office. Patricia wasn't there but that wasn't unusual since Janae left before. She'd spent her lunch break sitting in the park around the corner and eating a sandwich. It was refreshing. When her break was over, she'd dreaded going back into work. She hated that feeling. Getting settled back into work, her office phone rang.

"Hi Janae. This is Patricia. Can you come to HR?"

"Sure," Janae said.

Puzzled, she straightened herself up and headed to HR. This had to be about the lawsuit. Her nerves started to get the best of her as she got closer. Though she was suing them, she hated conflict. The world should be fair and conflict-free. That's what made her happy. Breathing in and out, she stood by the door. Finally, she got the nerve to knock. She was summoned to come in. Walking in, she saw the Human Resource Manager and Patricia.

"Have a seat," said Lydia, the HR manager.

"Ok," Janae said as she sat in a seat facing Lydia. Patricia was seated almost next to her.

After too long of a silence, Lydia finally spoke.

"I wasn't aware that you were having issues with our organization," Lydia said. "Not until we received court papers today. You're suing us for racial discrimination? You never came to me and complained about anything, which is the only way to know what's going on and help you out."

"Sorry I didn't come personally to you but since Patricia is my boss, I spoke with her. She is aware of how I feel and why I feel that way. She has issues with my hairstyles, and I can't meet clients who love my work and ideas and it's all because I'm black. How am I supposed to feel about that?"

Lydia tried to keep her composure as she glanced at Patricia. It was obvious that Patricia hadn't told her everything.

"Is there anything you'd like to say Patricia?" Lydia asked her.

"Just that I haven't discriminated against her and I told her she would meet the client soon." Patricia looked at Lydia but not Janae.

"So, you didn't discriminate against my hair?" asked Janae.

Patricia didn't say anything. Lydia looked at her, but she still didn't say anything.

Lydia sighed, "Well, I can't be sure what was or wasn't said because you didn't tell me. If you feel you're being discriminated against, it is only fair to give our organization a chance to correct things. But, you didn't. You chose to do a lawsuit."

Janae remained quiet but continued to look at Lydia.

"Unfortunately, you leave me no choice. We love your work, but you filed a lawsuit without even talking to me about anything. Unless you drop the lawsuit, we have to let you go." Lydia looked sympathetic but Janae knew better.

"So, I'm fired for standing up for myself against my boss? I answer to her. It was her job to talk with you. Is she being fired too? She didn't tell you what we discussed but she should have since she's management. It was her place. She also criticized my urban hairstyle and discriminated against me. Yet, she still has her job?" Janae was puzzled and disappointed. Ashton told her this could happen, but she didn't think it would after all the hard work she'd put in through the years. She just thought it would be silent treatment and working her extra hours.

"Look, I'm sorry. You left me know choice. You didn't use the chain of command. If you didn't think talking to her was working, you should have come to human resources. We resolve issues and handle hostile work environments. But, you chose drastic action, and you can't work here and have a lawsuit against us at the same time. So, you have a choice. You can drop the lawsuit and continue employment here. Then, we'll address all your concerns and make sure you feel equal. If you don't drop the lawsuit, we have to let you go." Lydia looked at her matter-of-factly.

Janae couldn't believe her ears. They were trying to bully and scare her into dropping the lawsuit. It was obvious that firing her was retaliation which was illegal according to Ashton and Charity. But, what if she lost? Then, she wouldn't have a job or money to live off of. This wasn't an easy decision, and their prejudice asses knew it.

They were probably thinking the black girl needs her job, so she doesn't end up back in the hood.

"I was discriminated against in more ways than one. I won't drop the lawsuit, but I can have my lawyer call to discuss some type of mediation to resolve issues that I have," Janae was giving them a chance to work things out with her somehow.

"Sorry but if I have to talk with your lawyer then it won't work out with you being employed here. We have to let you go. We're offering two weeks of severance pay. I'll email everything to you. In the meantime, I need you to leave the office immediately." Lydia stood up,

"Wow, so I'm fired just like that? No addressing issues or investigating?" Janae was shocked.

"I gave you choices and you chose," Lydia said. "You have to leave the building immediately. I'll have someone box up your stuff and send to you."

"You can't send my purse, keys and coat," Janae said trying her best not to get smart, but she was perturbed at the treatment. "I'll be getting those myself."

"Ok but I'll walk with you," Lydia said. I have to make sure you don't touch or take anything from the company.

Janae felt humiliated as Lydia walked with her to her office space she shared with Patricia. She couldn't believe the treatment. And Patricia didn't have the audacity to say anything to her or walk with them. She grabbed her jacket, purse and keys. There was one picture she had of herself on her desk, so she snatched it up. She didn't want anything else in that place. After grabbing her purse, Lydia followed her out of the door.

"I can walk by myself," Janae told her nicely.

"Ok. Sorry about everything," Lydia said before slowly walking off.

Janae turned her head and walked out of the office. She didn't look at the receptionist. She'd never felt so humiliated in her life. In her head, she kept thinking how she couldn't wait to make them pay! Once she reached the car, she felt numb. It was after she crank up her car and drove off that the tears started falling. She'd put in hard work over the years, and it seemed it was all going to waste.

<u>Chapter 15</u>

After going home in tears, Janae cried a few minutes until she decided it was enough. Her hard work wouldn't be in vain. This gave her even more reason to fight. Right was right and wrong was wrong. Picking up the phone, she called Ashton. She told him everything that happened exactly how it happened. He was not happy with her treatment either. He hadn't expected her to be fired so soon. Once she was done talking to him, Janae hung up the phone.

Instead of getting her resume together for another firm, Janae decided to research starting her own freelance marketing company. If she hadn't learned anything else, she learned no one would look out for her like herself so why not put in the work. The plan was to start working for herself at home once she'd done proper research and figured out what all needed to be done. Hopefully, her small savings could help her get started.

~

It was later that night when Charity found out what happened with Janae. She hated how her friend was treated. It made her proud that instead of sulking and crying, Janae was going to start her own business. The situation also made her think about her job. The change in Mr. Peter's behavior was out of the blue. Of course, she was glad that she wasn't being written up, but she still felt that it was something going on that she didn't know about.

She was lost in her thoughts after hanging up with Janae. Briefly, she'd forgotten that Ashton was there. Him walking in the room reminded her.

"So, Janae just told you what happened?" Ashton asked.

"Yes. And you better get their ass for my friend," Charity told him.

"No worries baby. I will," he told her. Then he walked up to her and they faced each other. "Have you thought about my job offer?"

"I have but I don't know. Mixing business and pleasure may not be good," Charity told him.

"Remember there will be a contract. It will cover us both. You'll have your job whether we work out or not and I'll have a wonderful up and coming lawyer working for me and helping win my cases." Ashton's smile made her wanna scream yes then jump on him.

"I'll let you know soon. I'm still thinking about it," Charity told her new man.

~

The next few weeks had been pretty busy at work for Charity. There was another big case that she worked on for Mr. Peters. Katie had graduated but was still on receptionist duties. Charity guessed they hadn't made up a position for her yet. Today was business as usual. She pretty much kept to herself at work except when needed and she handled everyone professionally. She'd just come back from grabbing lunch. She hadn't eaten yet. Her plan was to eat and work at her desk.

As soon as she sat down and bit her sandwich, there was a knock to her office door.

"Come in," Charity said while chewing her sandwich.

"I'm sorry. I didn't know you were on lunch," Laura Reed said. Charity was surprised to see her. Seeing Laura always made Charity feel that something was wrong.

"It's fine. We can talk. If you don't mind me taking a few bites," Charity laughed. She was hungry today because she hadn't eaten breakfast. She also wanted to break the house because she felt something was wrong.

Laura came in and shut the door behind her. She sat in a chair across from Charity.

"I won't keep you long, but I want to talk to you.

Some things have been brought to my attention concerning Mr. Peters. I'm not at liberty to say what it is. But, I do want to personally let you know that we don't think you did anything wrong in the situation of the previous case. On behalf of our company, I would like to apologize for everything that happened regarding him trying to reprimand you. He's officially in the wrong," Laura told her.

Charity was kind of confused. "So, what has been brought to your attention? Does it have anything to do with race?"

"As stated, I'm not at liberty to say because of confidentiality. I will say not necessarily race but how he treats women overall," Laura said. "That's all I can share."

Many thoughts went through Charity's head. She wondered if Katie had anything to do with their change of heart.

"So, what now?" Charity asked. "Does he still work here?"

"Unfortunately, he is a partner so he can't be fired. He can sell and be bought out. But, you don't have to continue working with him. I can set you up with one of the other partners or I can pay you 6 months of severance pay for your grievances and you can use that to take your time and find another job. You can even start law school."

What. the fuck? Charity thought this to herself. So, no more working with Mr. Peters? She would have to find a new partner to work with? Or just leave with 6 months' pay?

"I know I gave you a lot to think about. I also know you've spent time working on a case for Mr. Peters. That's why your severance package is so good. You deserve to be compensated for that. We just need you to forward all your notes and work to Mr. Peters then your part is done. After that, you can leave for the day and take a few days to think about what I said. Do you want to work here with another partner? Or explore your options and get paid for half a year?"

"That is a lot to think about. When I walked into work this morning, this is not what I expected," Charity said.

"I understand. Take the rest of the day. We need to know by tomorrow. Call me so I know what to arrange," Laura said.

Charity left work. *Work with a new partner?* She thought to herself. *Would she get more courtroom time and more chances? Or would it be some of the same old bull?* Six months' worth of pay sounded good too. She could start fresh at a new company. She knew without a real plan that money could go quickly, and time would fly by. There was a lot for her to think about. Going home, she turned her phone on silent and thought about her life.

Chapter 16

One Month Later

It had been a trying month, but things had turned out better than expected. Currently, Charity, Janae and Ashton were to Charity's house celebrating. They were celebrating Charity getting into law school. Her days and nights would be long because she was still going to work with Ashton when she wasn't in school and on weekends to make up for the time in school. Some of her classes were online and that helped tremendously. It hadn't taken her long to decide to leave the job and take the six months of pay. Ashton told her that she probably had a lawsuit because of how Mr. Peters' treated her, but she chose not to sue. Court cases get postponed a lot and can drag out. Her love life was getting better, and she didn't want to deal with all the stress. She took the nice severance package, signed up for law school and worked for Ashton. The severance gave her a cushion and the ability to work less hours.

Ashton paid her full time pay anyway because she always worked nights and weekends when needed. They'd made a contract that worked in both their favors. He couldn't fire her for just any reason if they didn't work out. Her contract was for two years and she could cancel at any time, but he couldn't. Charity thought that was more than fair of him. It was scary and exciting to take the chance, but it was working out great and she was ready for whatever was ahead.

They were also celebrating Janae's win. Ashton had met with her firm's lawyers and they didn't want to go through litigation and possibly get negative press, so they wanted a fair settlement. Being that Janae was going to start her own firm and needed to rent an office and other expenses associated with it, they settled on $50,000. Ashton's fee was 10%. Janae had enough money to pay ahead some bills and start her business. It would take hard work to keep things going but Janae knew that she could do it. She was already working on branding. Being smart with her money, she rented a small office space to get started.

"A toast to the law school student and to our new business owner," Ashton said as he raised his glass.

Charity and Janae followed suit once they realized that he was toasting to them. They raised their wine glasses. After all the troubles and tribulations at their job, in the end they came out winning. They were blessed or what some would call lucky because in so many jobs across the world, many black people were being discriminated against. They were being underpaid, working harder and looked at different because of their culture. It wasn't fair. Charity vowed to help black people with employment race issues once she became a lawyer. Justice had to start somewhere.

THE END

REAL STORIES...

The short story you just read was a fiction story. But those type of situations or worse happen in workplaces every day. It's happened to me, my family, my friends and when discussing it, I've noticed that it has happened to many people. In this section, I discuss some of the real-life situations that happened (different names and businesses). Maybe if we talk about it more and if people can see how it affects us, just maybe it can stop happening.

THE FINANCE FIRM

Sarah'd been excited and nervous to start her job at the big firm. She had a degree and she'd gotten experience working at a construction firm. Though the work was similar, she was used to dressing down doing Accounting at the construction place. At this big firm, she'd be dressing up. Excited, she'd took her savings and went shopping for new work clothes so that she could fit in. It was odd enough that she was one of only three people who worked there. It wouldn't stop her from working hard and being her best.

At first it felt odd getting to know everyone. There were some people, particularly white men, in the firm who looked at her like she was a foreign alien. They'd speak to her but the uneasiness in their voice was apparent. The ladies Sarah worked with were pretty nice.

When Sarah came to work with her hair braided one time, one of her co-workers had the nerve to touch and say, "Sarah what is that in your hair?"

"It's braids," Sarah said.

"Oh ok," the lady continued staring at her hair. It made Sarah uncomfortable, but she didn't say anything.

In Sarah's area was Pam and Melissa. They were both white women. They all were Accounting clerks and held the same position. They did work for the Partners of the firm. Pam was in her late 50's. She was married with adult kids. She had many years of experience in this area. Mallory and Sarah were both in their 20's with 2 kids. Mallory was married. She'd started working there after Sarah. She didn't have a degree or experience but was lucky enough to still get hired.

Sarah had a degree and a few years of Accounting experience. She was a single mom of two kids. Besides the odd comments about braids, Sarah liked working with Pam and Melissa. They were the only ones in the entire company who made her feel normal, and they always told her how good of a worker she was.

There'd been a few days that Sarah woke up to sick kids. Not wanting to miss work, she'd always called her mom or grandma to look after the kids. Being their mother, this made her feel guilty. She would spend her days at work worried and checking in with her kids. Occasionally, she would call in if they had to go to the doctor.

At one point it seemed like Melissa's kids got continually sick. Though she had a husband, whom she told them wasn't working at the moment, she would call in. It got to the point when it was beginning to be every week. Sarah noticed that Melissa would call in on either a Friday or Monday. It made her feel that Melissa wanted a 3-day weekend, every weekend. Of course, Sarah didn't say anything.

Because of Melissa being out so much, Sarah and Pam were busier in the office. One day, Sarah was working on something usually done by Melissa. She went to her desk to find a file. While looking for the file, she stumbled upon Melissa's check stub. Glancing at it, Sarah couldn't believe her eyes. Melissa had no experience or degree but was making $4 an hour more than her! This outraged Sarah but she couldn't show it.

Why was she getting paid so low with experience and a degree? Sadly, she knew why. It was because of her skin color. Sarah didn't know how to handle it. She decided there was nothing she could do but take note of it and ask for a raise later. It really saddened her though. There she was making sacrifices and still coming to work when her kids were sick. Melissa missed more days of work than she had PTO but still was getting paid more than someone with a degree and who worked harder.

Months after discovering the pay difference, Sarah was still disheartened but that didn't stop her from working hard. It didn't stop her from liking Melissa either. They got along good. Pam was off one day so their area only had Sarah and Melissa one day.

"How are your kids?" Sarah asked Melissa. She was asking because Melissa had been out again with them just a couple of days ago.

"They're good girl. I just don't be feeling like coming here. I get tired," Melissa admitted.

"I feel you. I don't have much PTO though, so I try to save when I need it," Sarah told her.

"Girl, I don't have any PTO."

"Really?" Sarah asked. "So, you're not getting paid? Does that affect your bills?"

"Oh, they're still paying me when I'm out. I have a negative balance in PTO," Melissa said.

"Wow," Sarah stated. "I was short 4 hours one time. Instead of being allowed to make it up, my pay was docked."

"Really? Probably was that bitch Jenny. She doesn't like black people," Melissa said. "That's wrong. Next time go over her head."

"It was only four hours," Sarah brushed it off. It stuck in her head what Melissa said about Jenny not liking black people. She was the manager of their area, but she wasn't involved in the work in their area. She also acted as HR. So, if she didn't like black people, Sarah knew she was doomed. There were times when Sarah'd thought that Jenny was being funny with comments like "Sarah are you with your baby daddy?" or "I know you know about living in the hood" when they all were talking at meetings or potlucks. Sarah always brushed everything off because getting a paycheck and taking care of her kids were more important to her.

"Yea and she could have given it to you," Melissa said.

Sarah knew Melissa was right but didn't say anything. She just took in all of the information.

Several months went by and work was business as usual. Melissa was still missing days with no PTO. Pam and Sarah were both still taking up her slack. It was almost time for reviews and raises. Sarah planned to ask for a good raise. In order to make sure she received what she deserved, she continued to work hard and stay late. She even worked some Saturdays when needed. Her mom had to babysit for her then too. It was worth it to her. She was paying bills and buying kids everything they needed with no help. Child support payments weren't coming. Her overtime pay also allowed her to take them out of town on weekends to places like the zoo and amusement parks. So, though she was tired, it was worth it.

One day they'd heard about some big meeting at work. After the meeting, two people in another department were laid off. One of those laid off was one of the only other black people in the company. Now Sarah was the only black person in a company of over 50 people. She heard they may lay off a couple of more people, but she felt safe because there were only 3 people in her department, and they were all needed. If one had to go, it would be Melissa. Her pay was more with no degree and she was in the negative with PTO because she was always out. Therefore, Sarah didn't feel worried about possible layoffs. It was crazy to Sarah how Melissa got away with all the absences, but she was smart enough to know that white privilege was taking place.

Weeks went by and it was time for Sarah to meet with Jenny. She knew it had to do with her review and she was prepared. Meetings made her nervous, but she planned to keep her cool. And she planned to ask for a much-deserved raise. Right before the meeting, Sarah went to the ladies' room. After using the bathroom, she washed her hands and looked into the mirror.

"You can do this," she told herself in the mirror.

Arriving to Jenny's office, she took a seat after notifying the receptionist that she was there. It wasn't long before she was called into Jenny's office.

"How are you?" Jenny asked her. She looked worried.

"I'm good. How are you?" Sarah asked.

"I'm ok," Jenny said. "I'm going to get right to it. You have performed excellent during your time here. You've learned a lot and of course there's always more to learn. Unfortunately, we're doing budget cuts and had to cut salaries in each department. Because of your salary and lack of prior experience, you're the one we have to let go in your department."

Sarah was shocked. "My salary and my experience? I have finance experience."

"I'm not saying you don't," Jenny said unsympathetically. "I'm saying it's not enough."

"There is someone in our department with no finance experience. I'm not saying get rid of her. I'm just asking you to be honest with me about why I'm the chosen one." Sarah knew why but of course they'd never admit it.

"I'm sorry," Jenny said again. "Please take your things. We'll mail a separation notice. We wish you the best."

Sarah was dumbfounded. She couldn't believe it. Going back in her office, she kept her back turned to Pam and Melissa as she grabbed her purse and hurried out the door. Instead of taking the elevator, she took the steps one flight down. After getting in her car, she drove home. It was evident that she was the one being let go because of her race. It didn't matter because there was nothing, she could do about it. She had a degree, worked overtime, even came to work with her kids sick. Yet, another worker with no experience and who was always calling out didn't lose their job when it was time for job cuts. In certain organizations, they looked out for certain people only. If you didn't fit the color, you were looked at and treated different no matter your capability.

THE CHEF

Andre had worked in the cooking business for years. After putting in many applications, he'd finally gotten a job at this popular fancy restaurant. He loved cooking fancy food, so he loved the unique dishes he prepared. He was Assistant Chef. The Executive Chef was the manager and ran everything. His name was Jeffrey. He was an older white guy. Jeffrey still cooked certain VIP dishes but because Andre was so good, he cooked less and taught Andre to cook more of a variety of things. He took him under his wing and taught him everything he knew.

Several years passed and Jeffery decided to retire. He and Andre were sure that Andre would get his position once he life. It was normal to place ads and advertise the position to make sure they've looked everywhere so Andre didn't sweat it when he saw the ad. He applied as anyone else would apply. During the time they were looking for a replacement, Jeffrey only worked two days a week while

Andre held the fort down other days. He worked 6 days a week.

As weeks went by, Andre noticed people coming in for an interview. He was puzzled as to why he hadn't been called in to at least interview. In his mind, it had to be because they already knew his skills, that's what he told himself. Jeffrey's official last day of work came. They had him a going away party. Andre had to handle everything on his own as far as managing the kitchen.

He did a great job and the other employees like having him in charge. They felt it was easy to talk to him. Though he made sure they worked hard, it felt good for the kitchen staff to not have an intimidating manager.

After a month had passed since Jeffrey left, Andre decided to request a meeting with HR. He wanted to know when the extra pay for the position he'd been doing for the last month kicked in. It took two weeks just to get the meeting. Andre was baffled but he knew they were busy. Once he was seated in HR's office, he greeted the guy.

"Hello sir," Andre told the HR Manager.

"Hello," Mr. Ross told him also. "How can I help you?"

"I've been doing Jeffrey's position since he left, which I enjoy greatly. I love it. I was just wondering when a raise may kick in. How much of a pay boost is the position?" Andre asked sounding very respectful.

"Andre, I'm sorry. You didn't get the position. We have someone starting next week," Mr. Ross told him.

"Oh," Andre said. It was apparent that he was confused. "I thought since I'd been doing the position all this time since he left that it was mine. That's why I asked for more compensation. It's for all the extra work I've been doing,"

"We appreciate your work. That's why we allow all the overtime hours," Mr. Ross let him know.

Not knowing what else to say and not wanting to jeopardize his job, Andre stood up. "Ok sir. Thank you for your time."

Andre walked out disappointed but didn't show it. He faked his smile and got back to work. The sad thing about the situation was Mr. Ross made a face at Andre as he walked out. It was as if he didn't understand why Andre thought he had the position after performing the position for over a month after Jeffrey left. Even if he didn't get the position, Andre at least felt that he deserved a raise. He'd put in a lot of hard work his whole time there but these last few months he'd been working even more. Sleeping and working became his schedule so that things could run smoothly.

Andre continued working hard but thought about applying at different jobs. It was about a week later when he was introduced to his new boss. It was bittersweet. The guy didn't know anything. He spent the day asking Andre a million questions. Andre tried his best to work and train him. It was hard because the guy just talked. He didn't attempt to help or cook anything. It was a long and exhausting day for Andre.

Time passed and Andre still found himself doing everything. The new Executive Chef cooked a couple of good dishes, but his management skills were horrible. He expected Andre to help with everything and it was getting draining for Andre. It was especially hard since he applied for the position, didn't get the job but still was ending up doing everything without the extra pay.

Andre was exhausted when he'd gotten home from work that particular day. His plan was to shower and relax on the couch. He'd just gotten undressed to jump in the shower when his phone rung. He was going to ignore it, but something told him to answer it. Naked, he left the bathroom and grabbed his phone out of his room. He didn't recognize the number, so he frowned before answering.

"Hello?" he answered.

"Andre Jackson?" the caller said.

"This is him," Andre said wondering who the hell was calling him. He'd already had a frustrating day.

"Hello. I'm calling with Wyndmere Restaurant and wanted to interview you for the Executive Chef position? Are you still interested?"

Andre couldn't believe it. When he'd applied to Wyndmere, he didn't think he'd get a second look nevertheless an interview. Keeping his cool he said, "Yes, I'm still very much interested."

The woman and Andre set up an agreed upon time for the interview. Andre couldn't be more excited. His bad day had turned great thinking about his upcoming interview!

~

Work had still been crazy, but Andre didn't let it bother him. He planned to kill his interview and be employed in the position that he deserved. The day of the interview finally came. Andre dressed to impress. Walking in the establishment, it was fancy. He loved cooking fancy and unique dishes for this type of restaurant. Going to the front area, he let the person up there know who he was there to see. He took a seat and waited only five minutes before being ushered down a hall to meet with the people in charge.

The interview went great. He met with the Executive Chef who was leaving to work in another city and met with the Restaurant manager. They made it comfortable and asked him several questions about preparing signature dishes and managing kitchen staff. He answered all the questions with great answers, and he gave examples. It was obvious the staff was impressed.

"Well, thank you for meeting with us," the Restaurant manager said. "Jeffrey was right about you."

Andre was shocked. "You know Jeffrey?"

"Yes, we do. Even though he's retired, he comes in one weekend a month to help us out with occasions or his signature dishes."

"Wow. That's great. I had no clue he would keep working," Andre smiled. He knew how much Jeffrey loved cooking.

"Yes," the current Chef said. "And once I told him I was moving, he recommended you to us."

Andre was so surprised. He was also smiling good.

"And after talking to you, we see he was right. You're hired!"

"On the spot?" Andre asked in shock.

"Yes. Can you start in two weeks?"

"Yes, I can!" Andre said excitedly.

They talked a little longer about pay and other stuff. The pay was double what Andre was getting now and everything he deserved. He signed paperwork before leaving. He was so happy.

The next day, Andre went to work and put in his two weeks' notice. The new Chef was shocked and scared. A week went by and Andre was asked to come to HR. Usually, these requests made him nervous but knowing he had a better job waiting, he didn't care. He entered the office and saw the HR Manager.

"We're going to be sad to lose you," the HR Manager said.

"I'm sorry about that," Andre said. "I finally get the Executive Chef opportunity that I've dreamed of."

"Wonderful. We made a mistake not giving it to you here. Since we've already hired someone, would you take a raise and more authority? We would hate to lose you." He handed Andre a paper with his new proposed salary amount on it. Andre was insulted.

"Sir, that is barely a raise and quite insulting since you know I have a good position elsewhere."

"A position is a title. Urban Chefs don't usually make much don't matter the title." The HR Manager seemed sure of himself.

"Urban Chef? A good Chef is a good Chef no matter their color or ethnicity. And you pay by the color of the skin, but all restaurants don't think like you," Andre said. "Instead of working this last week, I just think I'll enjoy some time off before starting my Executive Chef position." He took off his apron and placed it on the desk. He wanted to throw his apron at him, but he was better than that.

Andre walked out of that job and smiled. Though he'd been used and humiliated, he was being blessed with another opportunity. He didn't want to think about how angry and frustrated he would still be if he hadn't gotten his new job. It was a damn shame that because of the color of his skin, he couldn't get the right recognition and deserved pay at certain jobs. He knew so many of his friends and family were going through this and had to just deal with it

until they could find a better solution.

SCHOOLYARD DRAMA

Unfortunately, racism takes place in school systems too. I have twin daughters who are now Juniors in high school. When they were in fourth grade, they were in the same class. One day, I got a call from the teacher that one of them was involved in an altercation. A white boy in their class hit one of my daughters. There was no consequence, they "talked" to him. Being understanding, I let it sly.

About a week later, my cousin's son was involved in a fight at the same school. Someone hit him and he hit them back. The boy who started the fight was suspended for 5 days. My cousin's son was suspended for 2 days. Even though he didn't start the fight, it was explained that anyone involved in a fight will be suspended. This puzzled me because my daughter had been hit and the boy who hit her hadn't been suspended. My daughter hadn't even hit him back. At this time, I thought about him being white and wondered if this was why he didn't get disciplined for hitting my daughter. Feeling uneasy but not wanting to cause trouble, I let the situation go.

Just a few days went by and my daughters came home and told me the same white boy in their class had hit another girl.

"Was he suspended?" I'd asked them.

"No, he just had to go to another classroom for the day," one of my daughters told me.

"Oh," I said, trying not to sound too concerned.

"This is like the third person he hit besides me," my daughter continued.

"What?" I asked. "And he's never been suspended?"

"Nope," my daughter continued. "That teacher let him do what he wants."

"That's not right," I let them know.

A few days went by and I got another call from my kids' school. My other daughter had been involved in a fight with the same little boy in class. I raced down to the school to get my kids.

"He definitely needs to get suspended this time," I angrily told the principal and teacher.

"Well, your daughter hit him back. She could get in trouble too."

"I don't care. This boy has hit both my kids and other kids in the class with no consequence. When my little cousin got hit and defended himself, he and the boy were suspended. I didn't think that was right, but I agreed with your rules. Now, you seem to be bending your rules for this kid. I'm sorry but I can't help but think it is because he is white," I informed them.

"That is not true. He's having issues at home," the principal defended.

"Many kids have issues at home. You don't know what's going on in my cousin's home and you suspended her child for defending himself. Rules shouldn't be bent for certain people. It is apparent he keeps doing what he's doing because he knows he'll get away with it," I furiously let them know.

"It's not like that," the principal continued explaining. "We will handle it."

"Handle it? My kids aren't safe. You are letting students get attacked and not doing anything. I won't stand for this. I'll be contacting the board of education. Now where are my daughters?"

No one said anything. The teacher went to get the kids and the principal walked off. As soon as I got home, I called the board of education and put in my complaint. Days went by with no response, so I emailed them to follow up and I included the principal and about five other people in the email. I wanted everyone to see what happened.

Finally, I got an email response from someone at the board of education saying the student had been suspended for two days. Several kids had been attacked and this boy got suspended for two days? It was unbelievable! As a parent, I didn't feel like my kids were safe at the school. Emailing back, I let them know how I felt. They informed me that they'd suspended him, and they weren't going to do any further action. Pissed, I talked to my kids about the situation. Even though I didn't condone violence, I let them know that if the little boy hit them again, they were allowed to defend themselves. They were allowed to gang up on him, if needed. Of course, it wasn't a proud moment having to tell my kids they were allowed to fight at school, but the school and board of education made it clear that they favored white students and I didn't feel like my kids were safe.

Over the next few weeks, I would ask my kids about incidents with the boy. There had been over 3 additional incidents. His punishments were sitting in another class in school, but he'd never been suspended again for hitting other kids. Ultimately, he ended up throwing a stapler and hitting the teacher in the face. He made her face bleed. It wasn't until then that he was kicked out of school. It didn't matter that black students were getting attacked by the little boy, they let him get away with it until the point that he ended up making the teacher bleed. Had they disciplined him before, that probably would have never happened.

My kids were only in 4th grade and got to see first-hand what racism was all about. At an early age, I had to have the race conversation with my kids. It didn't feel good telling them that some people wouldn't like them just because of their skin color. Though it can be subtle, racism is still very much present in schools and workplaces. If we recognize it, we must speak up about it.

IMPORTANT MESSAGE

There are so many other examples of racism in workplaces. Good employees aren't making it to the management level because some organizations don't believe black people know how to manage or they just don't want to pay black people the money required for a management position. There are situations where black people work in the back office because employers think a "white face" up front is more presentable. Racist employers hire new people with little or no experience to lead experienced and smart black people because they don't want to promote black workers. The examples in this book, real and fiction, had good endings. In all the stories, either the job was sued, or the employee was blessed with a better job. Unfortunately, there aren't as many happy endings in real life work-related racial discrimination situations. Black people are going to work miserable and suffering every day because they are scared to stand up for themselves, in fear of losing their jobs. Because of responsibilities and bills, people are dealing with disrespect and unfair treatment in workplace and it's making them miserable and unhealthy.

I've researched instances where employees would reach out to human resources about their mistreatment, but human resources would brush it off. Even if there was proof of the discrimination, most human resources managers won't help employees because they don't want to make their organizations look bad. Most of all, they don't want to be sued. Open door policy is preached in many workplaces but when it's used, employees can be frowned upon.

So, what do you do when you feel you're getting discriminated against? Who do you turn to if you don't feel safe with management or human resources? The best thing to do when you feel you're being discriminated against is evaluated and study the situation. Just because you're being reprimanded or don't like something your boss says, it doesn't mean they're racist. It could just mean you're not doing your best job, or you have things to learn. Racial discrimination is when you're being mistreated simply because of the color of your skin. It could be hard to prove. I recommend keeping a journal of every instance you feel that you'd been discriminated against. If you try to communicate with your manager about it, make sure you communicate respectfully and professionally. If you can email or communicate in writing, it would help. Once you have a written record to show discrimination, contact EEOC (Equal Employment Opportunity Commission) and file a complaint. They evaluate your complaint and perform an investigation into your workplace. At the end of the investigation, they determine whether or not they feel you have a lawsuit for discrimination. No matter their determination, you're always allowed to sue on your own. Before investigating, they try to arrange mediation with you and your employer to come to some type of agreement on severance pay or agreement to stay at the job if they promise they won't discriminate against you. No matter what the outcome is, your employer is not allowed to fire you or retaliate against you in any way because of your complaint.

In addition to racial discrimination, gender discrimination is big. Women get paid less and treated differently than men in many workplaces. Women are leading the household these days and it isn't fair that they aren't getting paid for doing the same job as their male coworkers. Other discriminations include age discrimination and discrimination because of disability. None of them are legal and EEOC can help you if you feel this is happening in your workplace.

Black people have a long way to go before we're looked at equal in workplaces. In the meantime, all we can do is work hard and make sure we do a good job and follow company policies and procedures. It would be hard to complain about discrimination if we aren't doing a good job and following rules because no matter what color you are, rules have to be followed and everyone in the workplace has to be respected. As long as you're working hard, being respectful and following policies, follow your dreams and try to reach your goals to be very successful. Follow the steps I listed above, if you feel discriminated against at work. No one deserves to get mistreated at work or anywhere else just because of the color of our skin. Black Lives Matter.

www.ingramcontent.com/pod-product-compliance
Lightning Source LLC
Chambersburg PA
CBHW020954160726
47994CB00006B/2213